BACK
to ZERO

Other books by Gil Rendle

Journey in the Wilderness: New Life for Mainline Churches

When Moses Meets Aaron: Staffing and Supervision in Large Congregations

Holy Conversations: Strategic Planning as a Spiritual Practice for Congregations

Multigenerational Congregations: Meeting the Leadership Challenge

Behavioral Covenants in Congregations: A Handbook for Honoring Differences

Leading Change in the Congregation: Spiritual and Organizational Tools for Leaders

ADAPTIVE LEADERSHIP SERIES

BACK to ZERO

The Search to Rediscover the Methodist Movement

Gil Rendle

Abingdon Press
Nashville

BACK TO ZERO
THE SEARCH TO REDISCOVER THE METHODIST MOVEMENT

Library of Congress Cataloging-in-Publication Data

Rendle, Gilbert R.
    Back to zero : the search to rediscover the Methodist movement / Gil Rendle.
        p. cm.
    ISBN 978-1-4267-4039-8 (book - pbk. / trade pbk. : alk. paper)   1. United Methodist Church (U.S.)   2. Mission of the church.   3. Theology, Practical.   4. Change—Religious aspects—Christianity.   I. Title.
    BX8382.2.Z5R46 2011
    262.001'7—dc23

                                                                                2011029415

Scripture quotations are from the Common English Bible. Copyright © 2011 by the Common English Bible. All rights reserved. Used by permission. www.CommonEnglishBible.com.

11 12 13 14 15 16 17 18 19 20—10 9 8 7 6 5 4 3 2 1

MANUFACTURED IN THE UNITED STATES OF AMERICA

To the grandchildren whose names
are already written on my heart...
Edward, Henry, Carolyn, Calvin, and Clara.

And to the generations of grandchildren
I wish my church to learn to make room for.

CONTENTS

CHAPTER ONE

WE'VE ALL GOT SKIN
IN THE GAME

This book is written for everyone within The United Methodist Church: members, clergy, district superintendents, bishops, and denominational, seminary, and agency staff—even people who are in sister mainline denominations—because we've all got some skin in the game. Having skin in the game means being invested, having something to lose. To have some skin in the game means that your own future depends upon the outcome. That pretty much describes all of us who are part of the mainline church in North America in a time of great and deep change. Some of us committed ourselves to be participants or members in a local church because we sought change and health in our lives, families, and communities. Some of us answered more formal calls to ordained ministry because of how our own lives were challenged and changed in ways we also hope for others. Some of us prepared for or were elected to specialized positions that we intended would help the church and therefore the people of the church. We've all got skin in the game.

When faced with great and deep change, we are all suddenly part of the same story. As a member or participant, I can no longer think only of my own personal questions and hopes. I am part of a larger community. As a clergyperson, I can no longer wait for my district superintendent or bishop to make things right, or at least better and more secure for me. As a bishop or denominational leader, I cannot wait for polity to be changed, for local church clergy and leaders to step up to new missional risk. The change in the mission field has already happened and is all around us in a postmodern world which is now global, deeply diverse, and rife with competing beliefs and value systems. As part of the same story, the same bigger picture, we all need to be in the conversation to address overall change and the need for a missional future within our established denominations and established

1

congregations, despite the constraints of current rules and past practices that have until now allowed us to neglect responsibility for new ways.

One of the first responses to baffling constraint, complex change, and dwindling resources is for us to shrink back into the part of the system where we have most control. Members and local church clergy find it increasingly tempting to become isolated, weakening the connection with the denomination, waiting for district superintendents and bishops or the general church to get it right for them. Bishops and conference staff find it tempting to shrink back into institutional problem solving and creating programs for local church development so that the local church can get it right and get more people involved. Meanwhile, national and global assemblies such as the upcoming 2012 General Conference take on a life of their own, shrinking back into political strategizing to elect the right delegates (for instance, those who will forward a particular agenda) and focusing on legislation with the hope that more rules will make it right.

A good deal of my consulting work over the past years has been with a fair number of our American bishops. I am struck by the regularity with which other leaders in congregations, conferences, and interest groups conclude their meetings with bishops by telling them that, as bishops, they should just "bish." In other words, bishops should just lead. It is a standard reaction in any organization or institution that when folks get uncomfortable or dissatisfied they go to the leader and demand leadership. Just lead. Just "bish." Make this thing better.

We all quite naturally want the leader to do what is necessary to remove the discomfort and the insecurity so we can go about doing what we know. But this is the same system that has built a full range of constraints that limit and restrict the ability of a bishop to actually lead.[1] We can no longer point to any one group of leaders and instruct them to change things on behalf of all and then either dismiss, or even enjoy, the ways in which it is impossible for them to do so.

Instead, we need conversation and conversational places across all levels of the denominational church where we can all talk about our shared situation. We all need to understand more and to talk more with one another about what is happening at the various levels of the local church, the annual conference, and the denominational church. We especially need to sit with one another across all of the parts of our denomination to discern and discuss what is happening in the mission field. As a leader, no one can any longer focus on his or her own part of the system, waiting and hoping that some "other" will address the larger issues. We are all in it together. We all have skin in the game.

Not the least of our challenges connected to moving into a fruitful future will be learning to break our own rules. I will say a good bit about rule breaking. Many of us like to think of ourselves as rule breakers, as creative people with spirits of independence. Others see ourselves as rule followers, knowing that stability and order lie in conformity. We watch over the shoulders of others and want to enforce compliance. The reality is that a revitalized future will require us to break our own rules. However, we will need to learn to do so purposefully and appropriately so that we do not dismiss the mission of our denomination or put parts of our community and connection unduly against one another. We need to learn how to honor the inheritance of our highly structured denomination and yet set ourselves free from the constraints of being so highly structured.

This book is about The United Methodist Church wanting to be a movement once again. If we are once again, as in the original spiritual movement that birthed The United Methodist denomination, to "spread scriptural holiness over the land," then we all need to be in this together. In fact, the essence of a movement is to commit to work toward a change that we all address together. If we are to be a movement we will need to claim a common spiritual task and connection that supersedes our differences. We've all got skin in the game, but that's not the same as all being committed to the mission of the movement. When it comes to the movement, there is still the question of who is in and who is out.

A Beginning Based in Scripture

If we are to talk about reclaiming ourselves as a movement it is appropriate to begin the conversation by grounding our considerations in Scripture. Movements need to be clear about who is in the movement and who is not. Movements need to be clear about their purpose and their wanted outcome. A helpful place to start is with the Gospel of Mark.

As a book, Mark appeals to me because of the pared-down logic with which the writer presents the story of Jesus. Not the richest in narrative detail, Mark is much more to the point. It is clear that Mark presents an argument about Jesus to the reader, an argument meant to lead to conclusions. I understand that experience is not always logical and linear. I have made much about our current time in the mainline church as a wilderness journey that requires wandering. This is not a logical or sequential moment in the church. Nonetheless, I can still appreciate a good straightforward telling of the story of Jesus that leads from the way the story is told to a conclusion—even if the conclusion is a difficult lesson to hear.

The conclusion is Mark 3:33-35: "[Jesus] replied, 'Who is my mother? Who are my brothers?' Looking around at those seated around him in a circle, he said, 'Look, here are my mother and my brothers. Whoever does God's will is my brother, sister, and mother.'"

Surely this was not an easy lesson for Jesus' family to hear. And surely they had a right to think of themselves as family—brother, sister, and mother. There is also a hard reality offered here that severely tests assumptions of relationships within the family of faith.

For our purpose in talking about Methodism as a movement, difficult questions about assumed relationships in the church may be the most appropriate place to begin. A movement is a group of people who intentionally, at their own risk, join together to make a change in the status quo. Being part of a movement is a choice. One has to choose to be in. We must each choose the relationship that any of us as individuals have to the purpose of The United Methodist Church. As the Gospel story makes clear, it is connection to purpose that allows us to claim relationship or membership. So we turn to Mark's compressed Gospel and the logical argument that leads us to the teaching of who's in and who's out.

Identifying Jesus

Mark begins with a section on the identity of Jesus that he tells through two stories of healing: the cleansing of the leper (Mark 1:40-45) and the healing of the paralytic (Mark 2:1-12). The argument here is that this Jesus is a different order of person and leader. Able to perceive the spirit, able to forgive sins, indeed able to heal the incurable, this Jesus is the Son of God. If the conclusion is about who is and who is not related to Jesus, it is important to first tell who Jesus is. It is fitting that this section of the story concludes with the exclamation "We've never seen anything like this!" (2:12).

Outsiders

Mark moves on to the section on embarrassments prompted by Jesus in the call of Levi and the eating with tax collectors and sinners (Mark 2:13-17). This part of the story underscores that in the eyes of others, this unusual man who comes from God pays attention to the wrong people. Leaders should speak to leaders; the god-like should address the godly. Jesus' chosen audience is an embarrassment. "I didn't come to call righteous people, but sinners" (2:17). Already, the question of relationships is being pushed and assumptions about those who are of God's kingdom is tested.

Rule Breakers

Then comes the section on breaking norms and rules (Mark 2:18-22). Jesus' disciples don't follow the practice of John's disciples and the Pharisees by fasting, and Jesus approves the difference. Jesus' disciples break the Sabbath by plucking grain to feed their hunger. The Pharisees remind Jesus about working on the Sabbath, but Jesus approves the law breaking of the disciples (Mark 2:23-28). Knowing that he was being watched, Jesus healed the man with the withered hand on the Sabbath (Mark 3:1-6). Jesus willingly broke the law, forcing the hand of the Pharisees to take a stand against him. It was as if he were trying to make people choose.

The Committed

Then Mark comes to the section on relationships, which is where the text begins to focus our own consideration of the church that would be a movement (Mark 3:7-35). Mark moves through a series of relationships that people claim to Jesus and that Jesus claims to people.

The great multitude (Mark 3:7-12)

By this time Jesus had attracted a great crowd of people. I suspect that these people fell into a rather long continuum, from those who saw him as a simple curiosity to those who saw him as the new hope for Israel. But clearly it was not about the crowd for Jesus. There is no need to have a clear counting of how many members are in the church or how many friends are on Facebook. Indeed, when tired or when needing to regain focus, Jesus regularly withdrew from the crowd.

The calling of the twelve (Mark 3:13-19)

Here, Mark recalls the appointing of the disciples. From the great multitude, there was a small group invited into a much deeper and more purposeful relationship.

The family (Mark 3:20-30)

Neither multitude nor disciples, the family of Jesus now comes into the story with their own assumptions of relationship. Apparently operating out of worry for Jesus or concerns about itself, the family assumes its right to make a claim upon Jesus to stop his foolishness. "When his family heard what was happening, they came to take control of him. They were saying, 'He's out of his mind!'" (3:21). Perhaps they felt he needed to be protected from himself.

The true kindred (Mark 3:31-35)

Here now is the context in which we need to hear the difficult teaching about who's in and who's out. Jesus was sitting with the crowd, teaching, when the family came again to call him away from danger and embarrassment. They were family behaving like family, assuming that they had claim on him. "He replied, 'Who is my mother? Who are my brothers?' Looking around at those seated around him in a circle, he said, 'Look, here are my mother and my brothers. Whoever does God's will is my brother, sister, and mother'" (3:33-35).

Crowds, disciples, blood relatives—who's in and who's out? Who is related and who is not? This Gospel teaching tests our assumptions. Those who are most related and connected to Jesus are those who share his purpose. This is where we need to begin our discussion of The United Methodist Church as a movement. People become part of a movement by choice, not by relationship or by assumption. It is more than by being one of the great multitude, more than being part of a small group called out from the crowd. In the case of a denomination that would be a movement, this suggests that those who are "in" the movement are not there by denominational membership, by role in organizational leadership, by ordination, or by appointment. A movement is a group of people who intentionally, at their own risk, join together to make a change in the status quo. To be "in" the movement is a conscious choice. It has to do with purpose, not with position.

CHAPTER TWO

WHAT HOLDS US TOGETHER

It is time to move ahead.

> Don't remember the prior things;
> Don't ponder ancient history.
> Look! I'm doing a new thing;
>   now it sprouts up;
>   don't you recognize it?
>
> —Isaiah 43:18-19

These words come from the prophet during the time of the Babylonian captivity. The prophet announced that God was about to destroy Babylon and a new era was about to be introduced that would change God's people yet another time. It wasn't God just solving old problems for Israel and returning Israel to its former ways. It was God about to do what had not been done before—and Israel would be different because of it. Yes, God had done great things in the past. At the risk of trivializing holy text, the spirit of the prophet's claim might be stated as, "You ain't seen nothing yet!" The warning was not to rehearse old history as if what was known from the past was going to, or should, happen again. Do not remember former things. Instead, expect the unexpected.

These are curious words for a people who constantly rehearsed what God did for them, and to them, in the past. Beginning by recalling the past was a formulaic need for a people whose continual effort was to gain perspective and to muster courage for their present moment. I wonder what the psalmist might write about if not permitted to preface all with a recounting of what has already been, with what God has already done. But here in Isaiah is the caution not to remember former things because something new will happen.

When something new is happening, we must let go of the old. This is

9

the situation of The United Methodist Church and of all mainline denominational churches in North America. It is time to move ahead. We cannot recapture or relive old strengths or rehearse old ways. God is about to do something new and it is, in fact, already beginning. "Now it springs forth, do you not perceive it?" For more than four decades the mainline church in North America has been trying to turn around its shrinking membership and loss of vitality. It has been a wilderness experience. In my earlier book *Journey in the Wilderness,* I recount the history of that experience and argue that the wandering in the mainline wilderness has been creative and important. We have learned more and more about what it takes to be Christian witness and Christian community in a changed culture.[1] But the wandering of the past several decades has been a way not of recapturing what was lost but of teaching us how to be in the future. The new is already happening. There is already evidence to point to. Hope is already blooming.

The Rhetoric of Movement

One piece of the evidence of the new is the way in which references to The United Methodist denomination as a "movement" have increased over the past few years. The rhetoric of a Wesleyan movement is gaining traction in people's speech. References to being a movement in people's conversation seem to capture what we would like to be as a denomination rather than what we have been. Yet the reality is that, despite our change in language, The United Methodist Church and its congregations are still long-established, large, bureaucratic institutions that live close to the traditional practices of earlier generations and lumber slowly to make critical decisions. The use of movement language suggests what many leaders would prefer to see rather than the institutionalism and traditionalism that still continue. We would prefer passion where there is organizational neatness, spiritual or entrepreneurial freedom where there are constraints and regulations, agility and experimentation where there is a staid culture of institutional dependency.

The increase of references to movement suggests obvious tension between what people experience and what they hope for. At the same time, the use of movement language also reflects experimentation, boundary pushing, and leadership risk-taking that is already happening. I argue that for some people language is beginning to change because it reflects energy and purposeful risk-taking that is already budding in our denomination. It is already springing forth and can be perceived. It does, however, require that we not be stuck in remembering the former things.

If the United Methodist denomination is to again claim aspects of a spiritual movement, then leaders and people will need to move beyond the mere use of the language and take seriously the behaviors and practices of being a movement. We will need to take more seriously the question of what a spiritual movement looks like in a mainline denomination at the beginning of the twenty-first century. Institutional survival can no longer serve as a purpose.

The Essential Center

Perhaps above all else our yearning for a movement may be a deep wish to recapture our center as a United Methodist people. We are a very large group of people with over 7.5 million members (not counting committed participants in our congregations and programs who are not seeking and will not seek formal membership). We are a very widely spread people across all of the regions and regional differences of the United States. We are a very diverse people ethnically, racially, politically, and socioeconomically. The fact that we are not as ethnically and racially diverse as we wish to be does not minimize the differences we already encounter. With such a large and diverse people, a search for full agreement (on language, theology, congregational practice, moral behavior, or political correctness) cannot and will not be reached. Like our individual congregations struggling with internal generational and socioeconomic differences, our full denomination will need to stop defining harmony as agreement. We do not need to fully agree with one another to be a Christian community and to share an experience of Christ that changes our lives.

However, what our efforts to be a movement can do is capture what now lies at the center of our denomination and at the center of our experience as United Methodists. Being in full agreement is not community just as always being happy with one another is not family. However, being connected to a shared and vital center that gives identity and purpose does make us one—one in community, in purpose, and in Christ.

What lies at the center of each of our mainline denominations has both eroded and changed over the history of the North American protestant experience. What was once at the center of each of our denominations was a specific and unique theology, polity, history, location, and ethnicity. Immigrants from Western Europe, in particular, came to the new North American land with the distinctions and identity developed in their earlier settings. Calvinists knew themselves separately and differently from Arminians and Anabaptists. Episcopalians knew that they were not Lutherans, and vice versa. These different people settled into different geographies in the New World, followed different rules and practices, and expressed their theology not only differently but often in opposition to the others.

The United Methodist experience was somewhat different since Methodism, both as a movement and later as a denomination, was a singularly American development without a European ethnicity or polity to hold immigrants together. Like all American protestant denominations there was an essential shared center within Methodism. This new shared center of Methodism was a theology and identity instead of a common geography or ethnicity.

The theological heritage and shared center of The United Methodist Church is recorded in the *Book of Discipline* in the section "Doctrinal Standards and Our Theological Task." Methodists from the beginning understood themselves to stand within the central stream of Christianity. We "share a common heritage with Christians of every age and nation. This heritage is grounded in the apostolic witness to Jesus Christ as Savior and Lord, which is the source and measure of all valid teaching."[2] Along with other Christians, Methodists believed in a triune God: Father, Son, and Holy Ghost.

Like other American denominations, the Methodists also claimed a unique difference for themselves among other traditions. In the section of the *Book of Discipline* that outlines our distinctive heritage as United Methodists we claim "the underlying energy of the Wesleyan theological heritage stems from an emphasis upon practical divinity, the implementation of genuine Christianity in the lives of believers."[3] We were, and are, a people who believe that God's grace, freely received, must also be married to the action of our lives so that our personal encounters of Christ in our own lives are expressed in responsible living and social justice. The particular thrust of the early Methodist movement was "to reform the nation, particularly the Church, and to spread scriptural holiness over the land."[4] Being a Methodist was and is meant to make a difference where we live. Methodists were connected by grace—prevenient, justifying, and sanctifying.[5] "For Wesley there is no religion but social religion, no holiness but social holiness. The communal forms of faith in the Wesleyan tradition not only promote personal growth; they also equip and mobilize us for mission and service to the world."[6]

The early Methodists developed their practical theology, polity, and history that would live at the center to hold them together in identity and practice. This early and clear identity provided a connection that went beyond the ethnic and earlier European inheritances that held other newly developing American denominations together. The Methodist connection was to mission and purpose. Through this clear theology and connection Methodists developed their own widespread geographical location and ethnicity. But unlike other denominations that followed European immigration routes by which Episcopalians ended up in Virginia and Presbyterians ended up in Kentucky, the location of Methodists followed the American migration of people in the new land as circuit riders accompanied or followed people in their wanderings. Unlike other denominations that carried a European ethnicity that distinguished them in language, accent, or practice from others, the Methodists carried the newly created and mottled American identity.

Nonetheless, in all of the various expressions of Christianity in the young America there was for each denomination, Methodist included, a center that held people together in identity and purpose.

Clear centers, however, can fade over time. By the end of the nineteenth century, Methodist theology "had become decidedly eclectic" with much less of a Wesleyan influence. This paralleled a decline in the influence of European theological tradition in other denominations.[7] A new, simpler, American theology that did not seek to emphasize or honor differences that were once so important was taking hold. What started with fever and passion as a Methodist movement matured, as do all movements that last, along an organizational life cycle. It became an institution.

Methodism was part of a progression in the history of American denominations that moved through the early stage of congregational confederacies where individual congregations clung to one another out of shared history and identity to mature into an organizational bureaucracy.[8]

The Initial Denominational Center
· Theology
· Polity
· History
· Location
· Ethnicity

Maturation into an organizational bureaucracy continued to power the Methodist movement. Denominational complexity developed. Where once John Wesley was, himself, the original and sole extension minister appointed beyond the local church in order to serve the denomination, his efforts were eventually and necessarily replaced and multiplied by the development of other boards, agencies, and specialists. In the early moments of Methodism, Wesley met the needs of the new denomination himself by being author and publisher, fundraiser, chaplain, polity regulator, and pastor to pastors.[9] As the movement grew in size and complexity, Wesley's singular efforts needed to be organized and delegated, thus creating a stream of agencies and organizations.

Parachurch expressions in a number of our American denominations formed into multiple examples of home and foreign mission boards, publication houses, Sunday school agencies, prison ministries, and chaplaincies as external agencies grew to meet the needs of the denominations. These external groups were eventually brought "in-house" to become part of the formal denominational organization. A number of our American denominations now struggle with the inheritance of these early efforts that were melded together in developing denominational bureaucracies. These missional units commonly brought with them their own boards of directors, programs, and staff which once served the specific purpose of the parachurch organization but which now competed within the denomination for resources and agendas to preserve their own purposes rather than focus on the full mission of the denomination. Nonetheless, the inclusion and development of a more complex and specialized array of departments, boards, agencies, and programs was more than a necessary evil; it was a strategic and missional necessity.

As in all maturing businesses, corporations, and institutions, growth and complexity demanded organizational attention. What was once an upstart organization's sole focus on mission and outcomes began to refocus internally on resources and processes as time went on. In his book on deep change Robert Quinn makes the critical observation that long-established and complex organizations eventually become a constituency of constituencies—a gathering of related subgroups that all have roles in the accomplishment of the stated mission.[10] Eventually such established and complex organizations develop both what he refers to as a public mission and a private mission. The private mission is the satisfaction of the strongest of the constituent voices in the system. So while the public mission statement of a school might be the education of children, over time the private mission of the school is to satisfy the strongest of the competing voices, which are the constituents of the teachers, the administrators, and the parents.

Within long-established and complex denominations the strongest constituent voices over time became the clergy, the congregations, the boards and agencies, and, by the mid-1900s, the interest and caucus groups of the denomination. Along with the development of these competing constituent voices three things converged to shift the center of our established mainline protestant denominations:

1. Individual and unique theologies became much less distinctive as denominations became Americanized and eclectic;
2. The increasing complexity of denominational bureaucracies naturally shifted their attention from external mission to internal institutional structure, resources, and processes;
3. The denominational economy changed as available resources began to shrink with aging membership, lack of growth, and rising expenses and demand.

As a complex and mature institution the United Methodist denomination, along with sister denominations, has quite naturally developed its public and private missions. The public mission of The United Methodist Church is now clearly stated as "to make disciples of Jesus Christ for the transformation of the world."[11] Indeed, I believe that much of the interest in reclaiming ourselves as a movement and efforts to reinvent the meaning of connectionalism stem from a deep desire to realign ourselves with our public mission. However, we still have the persistent private mission of satisfying constituent voices that compete over denominational resources of attention, structure, dollars, and importance. As competing constituent voices clergy quite naturally want to be sure that their appointments are secure and satisfying, congregations quite naturally want to be sure that they have leadership that satisfies their needs, boards and agencies quite naturally want budgets to support their growing expenses, and interest groups quite naturally want attention and resources directed to the issues closest to their hearts.

Where once theology and history claimed the center that held people and congregations together, the denomination matured into a new institutional center much more directly driven by constituent demands and organizational needs. The new center might more realistically be identified as follows.

The Initial Denominational Center	The Institutional Denominational Center
· Theology	· Appointments (clergy deployment)
· Polity	· Regulatory polity that manages competition by enforcing rules
· History	· Pension costs
· Location	· Health insurance
· Ethnicity	· Mission that goes beyond the capacity of the local church

The old center that encouraged shared identity and purpose has largely been replaced with a new center focused largely on institutional needs.

The transition of denominational centers from the early stage of a movement of circuit riders taking scriptural holiness across the land to the later stage of complex and orderly institutional bureaucracy served The United Methodist Church well from the 1800s to the 1950s. We negotiated the expansion of the American nation and major periods of national and religious growth, and we began our attempt to negotiate diversity and racial inclusiveness. We moved, along with others, from separate identities to a newly developing American character. We moved, along with other businesses, trades, and institutions, from a collection of cottage industries to an organized manufacturing and service force that believed in continual progress and growth. We did well in an expanding economy (although there were period setbacks in the national history).

However, our mission field has shifted again. From a local to a regional to a national people, we now live in a global community. From an established North American Protestantism comfortable with the Judeo-Christian neighbors, we now speak of faith in a multireligious landscape amid voices of competitive religious and nonreligious values that invite people into a mosaic of self-understanding. Technology has changed the way we communicate, learn, shape identities, and build community. The rapid and deep change that we have been through in past decades is a complex story both well known and still being discovered.

Among the results of these deep changes is the reality that our neat institutional centers are no longer adequate to hold us together. Being united through the denominational operations of the appointment process, apportionments, pensions, and health care may be an organizational necessity, but it does not carry the character of our mission, our identity as a people, and the purpose of who we are now as a people of God. We are seeking more.

What we have at the moment is the connection of a strained membership. We all, somehow, belong to the same denomination—and the terms of membership and connection are being tested. Do we all need to agree on the specifics of theology, social witness, and moral boundaries? Do we all need to worship in the same way, and if latitude is possible, what are the limits to be observed? Do we all have to pay apportionments in full if we are stretched with the costs of our own local church or the opportunity of local ministry? Do we all need to support mission and caring ministries through our denominational channels, or are we free to make a difference in the world as directed by our own interests and passions?

The same strain felt at the denominational level in the relationship between local church and denomination is experienced in the congregational relationship between people and the local church.[12] Do people need to find all of their spiritual needs met in one congregation, or can that one congregation be part of a larger matrix of spiritual communities that help shape the person's spirit? Can a commitment of prayers, presence, gifts, and service be lived without a strict institutional connection to only one congregation or one denomination? Can spiritual disciplines be practiced beyond the local tradition, and can they be shared with seekers who are not part of the same congregation, denomination, or faith tradition?

The Essential Connection

We are a covenantal people. We express our relationships to one another as promises—a covenant agreement between the individual and the congregational community, between the local church and the denomination. The covenantal language of United Methodists is expressed as "connection." We are connected by a shared identity and a promise to belong to one another as God was connected to the Israelites in the original biblical covenant. However, because of the recent and dominant expression of our church as an institution we have currently defined covenant promise in very institutional ways—faithfulness to institutional polity, legislation, and practice; faithfulness through exclusive participation and financial support of the local church and denomination.

We need a new center. It is time to move ahead. It is not time to rehearse what God has done already in us as if the intent is to recapture, renew, or rethink who we once were and what we once did. God is already doing the new in our midst. Perhaps that is why we are so uncomfortable with ourselves.

We claim to no longer be an institution whose purpose is to make members. Instead, we long to be a movement that makes disciples. So we will, of necessity, have to reinvent the purpose of the local church and the annual conference. As noted in the *Book of Discipline*, the historic thrust of the early Methodist movement was "to reform the nation, particularly the Church, and to spread scriptural holiness over the land."[13] The idea of reforming the nation and spreading scriptural holiness over the land is always a pleasing thought. It can be a task that stirs the blood and leads to passion to reform a whole nation. To have found a better way and to want to tell and teach others about it so that their lives are changed, to have a sense of God's justice and announce it to a mistaken world, can be oh so satisfying.

For a long time I glossed over and dismissed a phrase in this mission: "particularly the Church"—to reform the nation, *particularly the Church*, and to spread scriptural holiness over the land. To change others can be satisfying, but to change oneself in the church can be difficult beyond measure. Yet, to live into the new mission to which we as a church now feel called, to be a Wesleyan movement, we must begin by changing ourselves. We no longer can afford to be constrained or directed by institutional needs and policies. So we will, of necessity, have to reinvent our connection and our connectionalism. We claim to be an institution whose purpose is now missional change, not self-preservation. So we will, of necessity, have to learn how to move beyond old measures of strength and create new measures of mission. To say that we want to become a movement again requires us to learn what a movement looks like in the twenty-first century, particularly if the movement is to be birthed by and live within an established institution. Movements and institutions are not the same. They do not naturally live comfortably together. Historically there is a political rhythm in which movements become institutions only to be challenged and sometimes dismantled by new movements. Can a movement live within an institution and provide new life and energy? We need to learn much, much more about being a community of faith in a rapidly changing world. To do so we will need to break our own rules of institutional behavior. But more about that in the next chapter.

So the question that we begin with is how will we be with one another in this time when we want to slip past our institutional constraints and claim freedom to address a newly framed purpose and a mission that is getting clearer? In the exodus the Israelites received the Ten Commandments so that they would know how to be with God as they slipped the bonds of slavery. As they dealt with the wilderness and the wandering, they organized and ordered themselves under Moses' leadership and Aaron's management into smaller linked units so that there was cooperation and cohesion. In the exile, when the Israelites were dispersed and found themselves in foreign lands, they developed the Levitical Holiness Code so that they would know how to be Israelites in lands where customs were different, tempting, and disorienting. In every time of deep change, God's people have had to decide again how they will be with one another.

To move from an institution to the passion, energy, and risk of a movement will require us, as God's people, to commit again to find ways to be with God and to be with one another in a new setting. If we take movement seriously, these will not be comfortable years ahead. Clergy and congregations will need to give up what has become an entitled dependence upon the denomination. Bishops, clergy, and agency people will need to vote against their own self-interests in order to move ahead. Congregational leaders and members will need to look beyond mere survival (even if that means losing their congregation) to ask and act on questions of a missional future.

There is a growing voice in the church that says that it is time to move ahead. "Don't remember the prior things." God is already doing "a new thing; / now it sprouts up; / don't you recognize it?" To move ahead with what has already begun will require us to challenge and change our own rules. Our future will become more difficult, as do all cycles of deep change as time goes on. As Christian community, joined in identity, purpose, and mission, we are all in this together. Change will not come by waiting for others to make difficult choices to move ahead.

CHAPTER THREE

BREAKING RULES

We can't solve problems by using the same kind of thinking
we used when we created them.

—*Albert Einstein*

No institution or organization has the capacity to break its own rules. Healthy institutional life depends on the organization ordering itself. Agreements, rules, boundaries, policies, and practices are all put in place so that complex organizations can be both effective and efficient. People and resources need to work together for common goals.

Once established, rules and policies are difficult to change. That is why companies, corporations, and institutions are routinely warned by their human resource departments to avoid setting policy to correct or control the behavior of a single individual who is creating a problem. The new rules may provide some leverage in working with the problem person, but when they become policies that apply to everyone, they create more problems than they solve. Bad behavior may be hard to change but not so hard as trying to change policies after they are established and applied to all. Institutions and corporations easily can make new rules but do not have the natural capacity to break those rules once they are made.

This is particularly true in legislative-based institutions like mainline denominations. Our United Methodist way of organizational life is set legislatively by the actions of General Conference, annual conferences, and local church boards and councils. We all representatively get to talk about the changes we envision and then we vote. We enact or we deny change through democratic practices. Changes are pushed or resisted by strong voices, interest groups, and caucuses, so any effort to change them back will be met with strong voices, interest groups, and caucuses. It is critical to note that in the United Methodist denomination there is no authoritative head leader with positional authority to make declarations and change the balance of competing legislative preferences. The Council of Bishops, where such authority is assumed to reside, is but one of a cluster of agencies each with power and responsibility for enabling and enforcing their own decisions but without power to provide direction to the whole church. Individual bishops play primary roles of following and interpreting denominational discipline and practice in their annual conferences, but they do not have the positional authority to change discipline or practice for the whole church. Local church pastors seek and need the approval of their board or council to make changes but cannot operate unilaterally. While each of these leaders or leadership groups can influence change, they cannot direct it. At each level of the denomination there are individuals, groups, or processes with either the right or the responsibility to challenge the leader if legislation, policies, and traditional practice are not upheld and followed.

Our denominational life has become more regulatory than missional. We have become a rule-following people. As we ordered ourselves through the continued addition of new rules over time, books of denominational polity such as the *United Methodist Book of Discipline* and the *Presbyterian Book of Order* have exploded in size and complexity through continual legislation. From the mid-1940s to the end of the century the physical size of books of polity grew exponentially as they became longer and longer volumes of cross-referenced complexity. The growth of denominational polity mirrored and kept pace with that of other nonchurch books of regulations such as the Internal Revenue Code and health care industry rules during this same period of time. The American people were finding new ways to organize and manage their personal and communal lives, and the new ways involved complex rules.

By the latter part of the twentieth century the effect of such orderly and ordered life began to be experienced as constraint in a technologically quickened world that required agility and personalization. Legislation and the legislative process shifted from a way to order our lives together to a way in which constituent voices competed with one another for attention, resources, or authority in constrained systems. United Methodists began to experience being rule-bound. Because our learned way of decision making was through democratic legislation we tried to change ourselves, recover vitality, increase effectiveness, enact social justice, and build community by increasing the number and complexity of rules and requirements developed at the denominational, conference, and local church levels. It has taken a good bit of time for leaders to understand that additional rules will not set a rule-bound people free. The insight commonly attributed to Albert Einstein fits well—we can't solve problems by using the same kind of thinking we used when we created them.

Rather than additional rules, we need bold people. While organizations do not have the capacity to break their own logjam of rules and norms, individuals do. However, individual rule breakers have a difficult task. They must be focused on purpose and mission and seek to honor the very rules they break, boundaries they cross, and normative practices they change. The purpose of this chapter is to explore how individual leaders must break rules purposefully and responsibly if we want to create a spiritual movement again.

Back to Zero

Many of us are familiar with the idea of paradigm shifts from the work of Thomas Kuhn.[1] A paradigm is a set of assumptions, norms, and practices that determine what we do and how we understand the world we live in. Paradigms are formed by our own and our inherited experiences that tell us how the world works and what we can expect in the future. Because paradigms are frames by which we understand the world and are tested daily by our experience, they are exceptionally durable. Paradigms often last beyond their usefulness because of their durability, but when they change the shift is usually sudden and disorienting.

Starting in the 1970s the public awareness of shifting paradigms grew as revolutions continued to surface in the physical sciences, technology, communications, and cultural and generational values. Kuhn notes that while we assume that progress and growth are linear experiences in which each additional day and year is an extension of the past days and years, there are times when, far from linear and progressive, change is disruptive, jumping to new insights and new levels, disconnecting from old ways, and challenging us to new thoughts, assumptions, and behaviors. We began to be aware of the depth of the shift by which organizational and cultural change no longer came from the top down (conforming to assumptions of the hierarchy of power and wisdom) but rather from the bottom up.

The United Methodist Church is in just such a paradigm shift, a non-linear jump of mission in North America. In this time we must think differently, behave differently, and even risk our security to move beyond our own self-interests in faithfulness. When a paradigm shifts, everything goes back to zero. Former practices are found to be ineffective. Old rules don't apply.

In my work with bishops and district superintendents, I have continually suggested that these leaders read and use their *Book of Discipline* in somewhat different fashion than normative rule following. Applying "back to zero" principles, it is appropriate for our leaders, clergy, and laypersons to read the *Book of Discipline* very carefully to find the separate purpose statements embedded in each of the sections—and then to stop reading.

An example is the disciplinary description of the charge conference, the annual meeting of congregational leaders with the district superintendent. The *Book of Discipline* states that the purpose of a charge conference is to "be the connecting link between the local church and the general Church."[2] Surrounding that basic purpose statement for a charge conference, the *Book of Discipline* then goes on for nine pages listing 44 separate legislative or administrative issues and functions applied to a charge conference. Many of the issues and functions are administrative in character. It is a long list that is the product of the legislative process of an institution over a number of years. Many of the issues will not apply in any given charge conference. Yet, the purpose statement is simple and clear. The charge conference is to be a meeting in which the local church (represented by congregational leaders) is to connect with the General Church (represented by the district superintendent). The essential question to be addressed by a charge conference is whether a connection has been made and sustained. Has the district superintendent listened to the hopes and the fears of the local church? Does local church leadership understand and work toward the essential purpose of the denomination?

The charge conference can be seen better as a missional conversation rather than as an administrative meeting. Its purpose is to make, support, and sustain a fundamental connection of mission and ministry. Such annual gatherings would not do well to be standardized across all churches, since not all churches need the same attention to the connection between the local and general church. In a local church that is in a transitional moment needing to ask deep missional questions, the charge conference may be a full day-long gathering of truth telling and discernment followed by an additional three brief conversations over the next six months between the district superintendent and leaders for accountability and support. In another church in which there is little evidence of interest or ability to develop a deeper connection with mission or the denomination, the charge conference might either be scheduled every two or three years or might be an hour-long meeting to pray for the people of the church, to remind them of a larger mission and to share a cup of coffee. For the bulk of other congregations in the district, the charge conference might be a regional meeting to share local stories of mission and experiments of ministry to encourage, uplift, and remind churches of one another and of their connection to the larger church. A district superintendent would do better to consider the purpose of the charge conference and what is required to connect any and each of these congregations to the identity and mission of the denomination. Administrative checklists need not be involved. Yet, despite being both strategic and purposeful, such an array of different formats for charge conferences breaks rules, both legislative and normative.

Luckily, even more than a Methodist heritage of discipline and order, ours is a Christian heritage of breaking rules. In the Gospel text, Jesus would be reminded of the Hebraic code only to respond with a better, more faithful way. When challenged by the Pharisees because his disciples, hungry on the Sabbath, plucked heads of grain, Jesus responded by saying that the Sabbath was made for humankind, not humankind for the Sabbath (Mark 2:23-28). Such stories of the relationship between Jesus and the law are multiple.

The Inferior Way of Following Rules

There are times in which breaking rules is the better path and such times have been experienced before. Such a time is described in the book of Philippians. Once in my personal reading, I came across the title "The Inferior Way of Following Rules" to describe the third chapter of

Philippians. The subject of the Philippian text was whether Gentile believers were to be required to submit to circumcision. Paul's target audience in the letter was a group of rival missionaries all offering their perspective on the rules to accept new people into the Christian movement. Most often when reading Paul, I think of him as a singular presence. After all, these are the *Pauline* letters. But there were other, competing voices to rival Paul, such as Cephas and Apollos, who show up prominently at the beginning of the Corinthian letters. Each was offering opinions on the rules to follow, and circumcision was the shorthand for those who had the appropriate background, those who followed right practices, and those who fit the mold of the earliest followers of Christ. Indeed, these voices were describing Paul himself. To make that point Paul recounts his own credentials:

> I was circumcised on the eighth day.
> I am from the people of Israel and the tribe of Benjamin.
> I am a Hebrew of the Hebrews.
> With respect to observing the Law, I'm a Pharisee.
> With respect to devotion to the faith, I harrassed the church.
> With respect to righteousness under the Law, I'm blameless.
> (Philippians 3:5-6)

Whatever Paul was, he was the poster boy of what was expected of a rule follower.

After establishing his credentials, his rightness by the rules, he then makes his point with force: "These things were my assets, but I wrote them off as a loss for the sake of Christ. But even beyond that, I consider everything a loss in comparison with the superior value of knowing Christ Jesus my Lord. I have lost everything for him, but what I lost I think of as sewer trash, so that I might gain Christ and be found in him" (Philippians 3:7-8). The inferior way of following rules. Instead of holding to his credentials and his evidence of rightness by established rules and agreement, Paul tosses these aside. The next part of the letter speaks of pressing toward the goal. In other words, purpose trumps regulations.

Credentials and regulations are established for reasons. They serve an institution in their season. But there are times when the rules need to be placed in tension with greater need and purpose. People must put their eyes on the goal. There are times when choices must be made. Like Paul choosing whether he would put his weight behind right ways on the one hand or the goal of Christ on the other, The United Methodist Church has come to a point of tension in which leaders are, at times, asked to choose between fidelity to polity or efforts of institutional change; between adherence to Judicial Council interpretation or trying missional experiments aimed at larger goals; between entitlements or missional purpose; between security and hope.

A methodical people who live in a disciplined way, we do not have casual freedom to disregard the *Book of Discipline*. We can, however, allow ourselves alternative approaches. In private conversation with several of the senior clergy of the very largest of our United Methodist congregations, one pastor reported a corporate consultant's conclusion that our largest churches found a way to make it work in a broken system. The observation of one of these pastors was that these largest churches were able to do this because they followed the spirit, not the letter of the law of the *Discipline*.

Seeking alternative ways to address the constraints we have created for ourselves in our rule making must itself be a thoughtful and purposeful process. There are rule breakers, there are counter-dependents, and there are just plain old frustrated folks who want to yell out that they will not take it anymore. In other words, not all people who break the rules are of one kind.

The Responsibility of Breaking Rules

Movement rule breakers see greater purpose and therefore risk different behaviors or practices for missional ends. Many of our local church, conference, and denominational leaders like to see themselves in such light, as do I. To be a rule breaker is to be courageous; it is to be creative; it requires insightfulness. Many of us like to see ourselves this way. Nonetheless, some discernment of our own motives and actions is appropriate before assuming the mantle of courageous, creative leader.

Courage, independence, and personal creativity may be the reasons given by a pastor for why he behaves unilaterally, without approval of the church board, or for why she absents herself from district clergy gatherings that she sees as purely administrative requirements. Creativity and insight-fulness might be claimed by a district superintendent who doesn't do annu-al interviews of all clergy in the district. A claim to hold the big-picture reality that others can't see might be used to explain why a bishop or gener-al agency executive does not comply with a regulation. We like to see our-selves in such bold roles as the person who will risk the rules for some other end. Nonetheless, we need to wrestle with pride, self-deception, and per-haps even laziness if the end result of breaking a constraint is to have the effect of increasing ministry instead of simply making less work for our-selves or relieving personal stress.

One of my favored memories of my time on staff at the Alban Institute was a casual bagel-and-coffee conversation with colleagues at a café. The conversation turned to naming the ten best books used most badly. We were reflecting on our experiences of how really good ideas could be, and were, misused for personal reasons. Quickly, the Bible went to the top of the list, with few explanations needed. Then we began to share experiences from working with congregations and their leaders. One of us noted the impor-tant concept of the "nonanxious presence" from Edwin Friedman's work in applying family systems theory to congregations. The nonanxious presence is that person who manages his or her own anxiety in a way to provide a calm presence as a leader. An important idea from an important book. Such a presence is essential in a system where people are becoming increas-ingly anxious to the point of not functioning well. Then the colleague told the story of when a pastor arose from the board table during a contentious meeting with leaders to declare that it was 9:00 p.m. and that he was a "nonanxious leader" who would not be moved by their threats and so was going home to his wife. In fact, he was not trying to help. He simply no longer cared if he offended the other leaders in the church. It was a good book used badly.

Another colleague recalled a pastor who was a self-declared alcoholic who carried a sense of pride about his disease. Drawing on Henry Nouwen's writing about Jesus as the wounded healer who provided wholeness by unwrapping his own wounds, this pastor drew on this important insight into the divine humanity of Jesus to claim that he maintained his affliction so that he could connect pastorally to the people in his parish. As we gath-ered around coffee we were able to provide a growing list of good books used in self-deceptive ways. We do at times deceive ourselves, giving greater purpose to our actions that may, in fact, be designed to make life easier on ourselves. Not all leaders are noble. Not all rule breakers are the same. We must discern our own needs and evaluate our own motives.

The Criteria for Breaking Rules

Beyond personal gratification or comfort, rule breaking requires a thoughtfulness that addresses purpose. Indeed, rule breakers will want to consider criteria for breaking rules since there should be as much discipline in breaking rules as in following them. In speaking of his own leadership in a military culture, a retired Army general offered his own discipline for breaking rules. He noted that a military leader might face a situation in the field or while developing strategy where new direction needs to be taken, despite the strict chain of command that set the original course. The general pointed out that leaders may need to break rules; however, they cannot act unilaterally, lest such action encourage a culture of rule breaking among soldiers. Instead leaders must progress methodically and thoughtfully. He noted the three questions that he used as a general to discern right action in such situations. The three questions are:

- What is the purpose of the rule?

- Is this rule still appropriate?

- Does the rule serve or prevent the mission?

As one would imagine, a military leader would naturally speak with an appreciation of bureaucracies and see them as necessary, because they provide transparent processes that allow repetitive actions and decisions already known to the organization to function without slowing the organization down. However, when it comes to new situations requiring new decisions, the general noted that bureaucracies "don't do new or fast well." In such settings the people closest to the action must make new decisions. Purposeful, missional questions are critical for making decisions in a discerning way. If rules are to be broken, there must be a reason, and the reason must be missional.

If a rule is determined to not be missional, the leader is still not free to act unilaterally. The leader is first obligated to change the rule. In the military, seeking such change might be managed by addressing a superior or group of colleagues. A response might be received quickly. In local United Methodist churches, where governing boards meet only monthly, annual conferences meet only yearly, and General Conferences meet only quadrennially, such appeal for change is rarely swift. Still, rule breakers are not set free to work unilaterally and spontaneously. There are other helpful steps.

One such step is the act of publicing. Publicing means that the leader states his or her intent to change or to vary from the rules publically before acting. Publicing is most commonly done with supervisors or with colleagues. A pastor does not have the freedom not to submit an annual list of local church officers and leaders, if such a report is required by the conference. However, the pastor can speak with his or her district superintendent in advance of the deadline of the required report and go public.

For example, she can explain to the district superintendent that in the coming year the leaders of the church have determined the next year to be a "Year of Jubilee." Instead of electing officers and holding administrative meetings, the church will meet for prayer and discernment about its future and its ministry. Holding a Year of Jubilee in which officers are not elected and meetings are not held breaks the rules. However, sharing reasons of missional purpose in advance is more commonly met with support and accountability than with old enforcements. The district superintendent is much more likely to support the efforts of the leaders and to add accountability by inquiring regularly about progress than to simply require a report for the sake of reporting.

A bishop who discerns the missional need for veering from a disciplinary rule or common practice would do well to public the intent with colleagues in the Jurisdictional College of Bishops for their support and accountability. Effective leaders must guard against change for nonmissional reasons. Since change of long-established rules and practices is subject to personal motive, it is both wise and responsible to approach such change prayerfully, with discernment and clarifying conversation with others who are in a position to give thoughtful feedback and critique.

Courageous and faithful leaders must confront old practices in order to move ahead. Such courageous and faithful rule breakers are needed in a time of movement, as rule-bound organizations and institutions are commonly limited to do only what they are already doing. Rule breakers are needed, but the idea of a rule breaker is not the best way to frame the leadership that a new Wesleyan movement needs. The identity of a rule breaker is a negative identity. A rule breaker is someone who stands *against* something. What movements call for are those people who stand *for* something.

Becoming a Citizen

What a movement needs are citizens. The opening decades of the twenty-first century find us in the political quandary where citizens—people who stand for the whole purpose of the movement rather than for their own piece of or interest in the enterprise—are few and hard to find. It is immeasurably easier to find those who stand against others without being clear about what they themselves stand for. There are many pundits, multiple interest groups, and large coalitions of defenders, but few citizens who will break the norm of self-interest and stand against old rules and old ways to find new, shared hope.

The work of Peter Block focused on developing community is instructive. Consider the distinction that he makes between consumers and citizens. Consumers are passive and dependent. They wait for the community to meet their needs. They follow the rules because accommodating what has been and receiving what is offered is the safest path, no matter where it is going. Citizens are different. Citizens are those people who serve and hold themselves accountable for the whole of the enterprise. Rather than seek their part of the resource pie, they focus on the need, the intent, and the purpose of the whole community, the whole organization, or the whole institution. Citizens hold themselves accountable to move the community, organization, or institution ahead even, if need be, with personal discomfort, risk, or cost.[3]

The distinction between consumer and citizen is thought provoking and a bit discomforting. When phrased as an either/or it has the feel of distinguishing between the sheep and the goats, where some are chosen and others are shunned. My experience is that most of us, including myself, are both consumers and citizens in some measure. There is a tension between the dependence we experience in the mainline denominational church and what we feel we were called to be a part of. However, at the time of recovering The United Methodist Church as a movement, leaders need to behave as citizens rather than consumers.

Perhaps the call to citizenship in the Kingdom of God is not as clearly felt by North American Christians because we have long been invited to be consumers in our denominations and in a consumer culture. Bishop Scott Jones makes the point that we have incorrectly made the distinction between the annual conference and the component people and congregations that make up the annual conference. He notes that we have allowed ourselves to see the annual conference as a form of parachurch organization that is meant to serve the needs and wishes of its member people and congregations, as if the conference is something other than a composite of those who make it up. When the annual conference assumes its purpose and mission is to serve the local church by providing leadership, training, and resources, it has fallen into the trap of being a provider of goods and services to meet the consumer needs of the institution and its people.

If the annual conference or general church is seen as the provider of goods and services, then we as individuals and as congregations are asked to assume a consumer position. The consumer position is passive and dependent. This is a familiar position in our culture, where we sometimes caricature "couch potatoes" who sit on sofas before televisions that become the delivery systems for a marketing industry that promises to meet all of our needs with few requirements beyond purchasing goods and services. Perhaps such an indictment is neither fair nor balanced for those in our consumer culture who seek self-direction and balance in their lives and are willing to be responsible for their own decisions.

Nonetheless the cultural disposition and the temptation is to want to be cared for by our leaders—politicians, teachers, doctors, insurance companies, manufacturers . . . and the list goes on. Many consumers who purchase insurance believe that they should not suffer from accidents and, in fact, look not just for recompense but for gain, with the assumption that their injuries should be cared for by others. Many consumers who speak to their physicians about medication advertised on television seek relief from symptoms or illness without assuming that there should be some discipline of diet, exercise, or self-care to accompany (or replace) the medication. Consumption as a value system leads us to dependence and passivity.

The notion that the denominational church is to meet the needs of the congregation, clergy, or members is an outgrowth of consumerism that invites dependence and passivity. Congregations often request training from their denominations in areas of evangelism, youth ministry, worship, stewardship, or conflict management only to make very few, if any, changes the workshop suggests. They put themselves in the position to receive the wisdom, information, and skills of the workshop leader without assuming that they need to do anything with the information that would require a change of behavior or strategy on their part.

The description of a passive, dependent consumer denomination approaches diatribe when stated so boldly, as if this was the given state of The United Methodist Church and the people in it. In reality, there are many people, congregations, boards, and agencies of purpose and mission who willingly take on responsibility for their own call. However, mainline denominations have a history beginning in the mid-1800s where regional, national, and parachurch groups were developed to meet the institutional needs of congregations and their people. Serving the local church and its people, in fact, routinely became the mission of the regional or national denomination. This then invited a passivity and dependence, as people were asked for little beyond following rules and conforming to established norms.

Citizenship is quite different. We are in a moment when many of us are responding to a call to the church. Citizens serve and hold themselves accountable to the whole of the community, to the mission of the church rather than to the institution of the church. It is spiritual, purposeful living that invites us beyond ourselves and our interests.

When a mainline denomination like The United Methodist Church again seeks to be a movement, it includes a call to citizenship. Change becomes purposeful. More than simply standing against rules that no longer work, citizenship calls for us to take responsibility to be purposeful. Leaders need to stand for something and hold themselves and others accountable for the development and birthing of that something. While consumerism and citizenship are both parts of our nature, if we want to be a movement, we must learn more about citizenship. When we clearly understand that there is new purpose to guide us, we are called to be citizens, following purpose over established institutional practices. The United Methodist Church has experienced such a new purpose in the shift from its earlier efforts to make more members to its new mission of making disciples. This shift is a new call that requires us to reconsider our positions within the church and their purpose. We have experienced a paradigm shift—a change so fundamental that it requires that we test our very values and assumptions about how we live and work. God is calling us to be a new people, to do a new thing, and it is time to testify.

CHAPTER FOUR

IT'S TIME TO TESTIFY

It's time to testify. Testifying and testimonies are, for many of us, an earlier practice willingly let go. One of my vivid and disturbing memories as a young pastor was to be a visitor in a congregation on a Sunday when confirmands were being received into membership. At a designated time each of these young people in their early teens was called forward to give his or her testimony. Each in his or her own way spoke of how God was great and good, how life was a veil of tears that one could endure only with God's (and the church's) help, and how only God could give release. I knew one boy rather well as being energetic and vibrant, constantly engaged with the fullness of life, and eagerly willing to try so many things, often to the point of getting in trouble. At times, I wished I had had such energy for life when I was his age. When it came his turn, this young boy ended his testimony by saying that he could not wait to die and meet God, who would receive him into a splendor that earthly life could not provide. I thought, I am done with testimonies.

In spite of my experience and its frequent abuse as a liturgical practice, testifying, with good theology, is legitimate and important. It gives voice to what God is actually doing now rather than announcing that someday, some way, God will make right all things wrong. Testimony, says Tom Long, is how "we talk our way toward belief. . . . Putting things into words is one of the ways we acquire knowledge, passion, and conviction."[1] Testimony is talking about what we believe God is doing in the present moment. When God's hand in our lives is making a difference, even a difference that is as yet incomplete, it is appropriate to announce it. I have long appreciated Bill Coffin's defense of miracles by saying that he has seen them. He gave testimony when he said, "I can only report that in home after home I have seen Jesus change beer into furniture, sinners into saints, hate-filled relations into loving ones, cowardice into courage, the fatigue of despair into the buoyancy of hope."[2] When we see God act in such ways, it is time to testify. The testimony may be of things not fully permanent or even complete, but it is nonetheless witness to what God is doing and of the change that comes from God's hand.

If that be the case, then it is time to testify in The United Methodist Church. We need to bear witness to a moment of *metanoia*, of repentance within our own denomination. Repentance is turning around, or going in a new direction. Having been going in an institutional direction, The United Methodist Church is now struggling to turn around and head in a healthier, different, missional way. The work is far from complete and will require effort day by day, day after day. Indeed, we are still at the point of simply understanding the change of direction. What we do know is that it includes the shift from institution to movement.

From Members to Disciples

The mission of The United Methodist Church is now to make disciples of Jesus Christ for the transformation of the world. This mission is newly named in our church only since 1996. Where once we made members, we now make disciples. This is repentance, turning around, moving in a new direction, metanoia. More than a shift in language, this is a deep and fundamental shift of who we are and what we do. Members are products of institutions and are needed for institutional life and viability. Disciples are quite different. Disciples are changed people, members or not. As changed people, disciples relate to their families, their workplaces, their communities, and to the globe in changed ways that will transform the world. Members are produced by institutions. Disciples and the communities and world that they change are produced by mission. God is doing something quite new and quite difficult in us. It is an act not yet complete. It is a transformation sufficiently difficult that it will be costly in what new things we will need to learn and risk.

This sounds shocking to the missionally minded, but as a young pastor, I was never trained to make disciples—only members. I was trained to change not peoples' lives but their affiliations. That seemed to be a task sufficient to the time when mainline institutional churches lived on membership. But God is doing something great and new in us and, despite the fact that it is only beginning and far from a completed act, and despite the fact that it is not yet clear that we will be fully able to make the change, it is nonetheless time to testify. The new direction that shifts us from membership to discipleship is a paradigm shift. It takes us back to zero.

Inputs, Throughputs, and Differences

Understanding the shift from members to disciples is critical. A beginning place to understand the shift is in thinking of the denomination as a system designed for some end purpose. Edwards Deming provides a simple model of a system.[3] There are three components to an organizational system—the input, the throughput, and the output, which we will redefine as the difference that the system is to make.

1. The input is what goes into the system. These are resources, and they are nouns. The input is to be used and is expendable for the purpose of the system.

2. Throughput is activities. This is what the system does with its resources. Throughput is verbs that act on nouns to create the difference.

3. The output, the difference, is what is created when our input resources are met by the activities and processes of the throughput. A simple system can be diagramed as follows.

INPUT	THROUGHPUT	OUTPUT / DIFFERENCE
Resources	Activities	What will be different
Nouns	Verbs	because of the verbs working on the nouns.

For-Profit Clarity

As simple as they appear, large systems are amazingly complex and difficult to manage. The simple system is complicated by management, human resource, and legal issues. Yet in for-profit organizations, the basic relationship is clear and can be measured. At its most fundamental, the input for a for-profit organization is money. Money is easily measured. It is an input that is needed to purchase raw materials, equipment, facilities, staff, and so on. It is measurable. The throughput may be quite complex and difficult to manage in a productive and aligned way, but it is a series of processes and productions needed to work with the input brought into the system. The throughput will be designed to make a product, whether it be toasters, automobiles, investment instruments, or surgical procedures. However, the final output of a for-profit organization is money. The output, or difference, is more money as output than the money used for input. Money is clear. One of the basic principles of systems is that you get what you measure, and it is a great advantage when for-profit organizations have such clear measures.

Nonprofit Challenges

The system gets interesting and difficult for nonprofit organizations such as churches and denominations. Nonprofit organizations do not commonly know what they produce. It has been said that the end product, or the outcome, of all nonprofits is an improved human being. True as that may be, such a difference is not easily measured. The lack of a quantifiable objective makes it exceptionally difficult for a nonprofit to be clear about the difference it is trying to make. What does an improved human being look like? For that matter, what does a disciple—a changed person—look like? We will encounter the difficulty of measurement continually over the next years because we are not at all clear about how to make disciples and how to measure the difference made as a person moves to become a disciple.

When nonprofits are not clear about what they produce and don't know how to measure their output, they measure their inputs and throughputs, their resources and activities. Clergy will tell one another how many hours they work in a week, how many meetings attended or visits made in a month, how many sermons preached in a year, how many books read. These are not people trying to impress one another with their work ethics. These are people measuring everything that they threw into their system hoping some good would come out the other side. Unable to measure the outcome of what they are trying to do, the alternative is to measure resources and activities. How many members do we have? Do we have enough money this month? How many people came to the Bible study? Reggie McNeil notes that the current dashboard measures for most congregations and denominations are "how much, how often, and how many"—all resources and activities.[4] It is not easy to be a nonprofit. It is not easy to be a local church, an annual conference, or a denomination.

The Paradigmatic Shift

Here is where it gets really difficult and exciting. God is doing something new in The United Methodist Church, and we are called upon to testify. The shorthand way of understanding the change is from members to disciples. This is a paradigm shift because the change from member to disciple is not a linear progression. One does not suddenly begin to make disciples because of improved practices in making members. To shift from making members to making disciples is a discontinuous leap that requires significant new learning, changed practices, and a good deal of risk. It is a different ballgame all together. The paradigm shift can be described as follows.

The Old United Methodist Paradigm

Outcome: more members; satisfied clergy; satisfied congregations

The New United Methodist Paradigm

Outcome: disciples (changed people who will change the world)

In the "old paradigm" we can fine-tune the description of the actual normative output of The United Methodist Church a bit more than just the metric of membership. An argument can be made that the output of the United Methodist denomination in the old paradigm was the making of more *dollars*, satisfied *clergy*, and satisfied *congregations*. More members were a desired outcome because they supported the institution and gave evidence of the importance, viability, and future of the church. The reality, however, is that the old paradigm United Methodist denominational system was built to produce not just more members but more dollars and satisfaction of leaders and members as well.

Satisfied clergy were an important product of the system that wanted to provide clergy with appointments to congregations that would seem acceptable to the clergy. The United Methodist institutional system sought to give every clergyperson an appointment to a church where he or she could do well and, over time, move to larger congregations able to pay larger salaries over the span of a pastor's career. Satisfied congregations were also important in a system that focused on its members. People don't join congregations that are unhappy. A desired end result was congregations that had clergy who could meet the needs of the people who were in the congregation, satisfy members' preferences for how they worshiped, and provide leadership for the programs of the congregation. In a classic statement under the old paradigm, one district superintendent stated that "as long as his clergy were happy and his congregations in the district were not complaining his work was done." The essential output of the old paradigm was more members, satisfied clergy, and satisfied congregations. Note how in the old paradigm the focus of institutional attention and resources was given to members, clergy, and congregations.

Understanding the paradigmatic shift from members to disciples means that the attention of the denominational system must shift as well. Not as obvious at first, but critically important, is the shift in the position of members, clergy, and congregations in the new paradigm system. In the new paradigm members, clergy, and congregations change their systemic position from outputs to inputs. Members, clergy, and congregations are nouns. They are not the difference the church is trying to make.

The Old United Methodist Paradigm

Outcome: more members; satisfied clergy; satisfied congregations

The New United Methodist Paradigm

Input: members, clergy and congregations.

Outcome: disciples (changed people who will change the world)

From output to input, members, clergy, and congregations have now been displaced as the object of attention and recipient of denominational resources to being the expendable resources of the system needed to make the critical difference of changed people who will change the world.

From Honored Outputs to Expendable Resources

Recently in a conversation with a number of bishops, clergy, and denominational executives about this paradigm shift, the conversation quickly focused on the idea of "expendable" resources. The group reacted with some surprise to the idea that clergy and congregations might be expendable rather than protected, preserved, or satisfied. After all, so many of the recent efforts of the denomination over past decades have been to find ways to meet the needs of members, clergy, and congregations.

Expendable does not mean the same thing as *disposable*. Resources are to be used, directed, allocated, expended for the desired end result of the system. Valued and costly resources cannot be cast aside. Instead, such valued and costly resources should be wisely used and thoughtfully expended in order to get the desired results.

Members, clergy, and congregations have a missional purpose. Helpfully, in the same conversation, one bishop offered a missional reminder. He pointed out that he fully expected and hoped that he would be personally expended for missional ends. What he hoped for, he went on to add, was to never be expended for institutional ends. For a denomination that would recapture a sense of movement, such distinctions are necessary. Many within the United Methodist denomination hope to recapture the notion of expendability that was earlier voiced by John Wesley in his prayer adapted for the service of covenant, first used in 1755.

> I am no longer my own, but thine.
> Put me to what thou wilt, rank me with whom thou wilt.
> Put me to doing, put me to suffering.
> Let me be employed by thee or laid aside for thee,
> exalted for thee or brought low for thee.
> Let me be full, let me be empty.
> Let me have all things, let me have nothing.
> I freely and heartily yield all things
> to thy pleasure and disposal.
> And now, O glorious and blessed God,
> Father, Son, and Holy Spirit,
> thou art mine and I am thine. So be it.
> And the covenant which I have made on earth,
> let it be ratified in heaven. **Amen.** [5]

Moving from honored outputs to expendable resources confronts the denomination with a significant learning curve. We are moving our resources from being the object of our attention to being missional raw material. Consider some of the shifts that we will need to learn our way into:

From objects of attention	*To* expendable, missional resources
· Use of measures of satisfaction such as few complaints	· Use of measures of intentional differences accomplished for missional purpose
· Clergy placement by tenure and avoidance of problems (egalitarianism)	· Clergy placement by evidence of potential or productivity (meritocracy)
· Denominational dependence and following instructions	· Missional alignment and entrepreneurial risk

Paradigm shifts challenge our assumptions and force us to reconsider our identity and purpose. Consider what happens when clergy appointments are made "to a particular mission field" instead of to a congregation. Under the old paradigm assumptions of satisfaction shaped the appointment of a clergyperson to a congregation. It was assumed that the clergyperson was to serve and satisfy the members and participants who were already present in the congregation to which the clergyperson was appointed. The goal of satisfying the people who were already in the congregation created an internal focus for both the pastor and the people who monitored his or her relationship as measured by the number of, or the lack of, complaints about the pastor. Does the pastor satisfy people's needs and preferences through his or her ability to preach, lead meetings, teach, visit, recruit new members, encourage stewardship—or a host of other tasks, roles, or responsibilities, all of which are to be managed in ways satisfying to that one local church? Similarly, questions are framed around whether the pastor's salary, housing, benefits, and community setting needs are being met. The appointment of a pastor to a congregation both localizes and internalizes expectations and behavior. Appointments to a congregation, while organizationally and bureaucratically efficient, lead to concerns heard over recent decades about congregations unable to look beyond their own four walls. Such is the power of assumptions and norms.

When the paradigm shifts and clergy are appointed not to the congregation but to the particular mission field in and around that congregation, assumptions and norms are challenged. Here the focus shifts from internal to external, from people already there to also include people not yet there, from care of facilities to concern about community, from satisfying members to discipling followers. If the mission field is understood as that place where God's presence and action are still waiting to be felt, then the mission field is not just the geography surrounding the local congregation's physical address. The mission field is also the hearts and minds of the people who can be found, either inside or outside the church building, who are in need of God's presence in a way that makes a clear difference in their lives. In appointments made to the mission field the criterion for a sermon is not whether the preacher manages not to offend those attending but whether the pastor is able to speak a word of meaning to people seeking God. In appointments made to the mission field the criterion for lay leadership is not just whether budgets are met and facilities cared for but whether the local church makes a discernable and describable difference in the community where it is located.

In the old paradigm, the output was members, satisfied clergy, and satisfied congregations. Good leaders under that older paradigm practiced managerial skills to make everything run smoothly. They focused on relationships so that members felt cared for. In the new paradigm, a new and different skill set of leadership is called for where purpose and identity become central and people are encouraged and exhorted to practice spiritual and personal disciplines to find a powerful change both in their lives and in their world.

An organizational standard, widely recognized, is that a smaller percentage of the people in any organization will effectively produce the greater percentage of wanted change or production. Known as the Pareto principle, it is commonly expressed as an 80:20 ratio. For example, in sales, 20 percent of the salespeople make 80 percent of the sales. Equally recognized is the effective organizational practice of directing 80 percent of the resources to the 20 percent of the most productive people in producing the wanted outcomes. Leaders direct resources and attention to the most effective parts of the organization in order to accomplish goals and produce output. Resourcing the weakest, unproductive parts of the organization with the hope of improving them has proven futile in organization after organization.

One of the most uncomfortable realities of the future is that as the paradigm shifts from the congregation to the mission field it will become increasingly important for the denomination to resource its best leaders and most ripe mission fields—the productive 20 percent. If younger, shorter-tenured clergy demonstrate greater potential or effectiveness they must be reasonably deployed to mission field congregations of greatest potential or effectiveness even if the appointment does not follow older norms of tenure in which all clergy, over time, expect "better" appointments and higher salaries. When paradigms shift the change eventually has real-life consequences that require us to work through the discomfort of letting go of old ways in order to respond to new situations.

Consider an annual conference that has historically provided financial support to as many as six college or university programs developed to provide campus ministry to young adults on as many campuses. In the old paradigm each of the six campus programs could expect to enjoy equal levels of financial support from the conference since equality and egalitarianism provide satisfaction and fairness in bureaucratic organizations. However, paradigm shifts that require clearer outcomes necessitate use of values different from fairness and egalitarianism. If, of the six, only two of the campus programs are effective at discipling young adults by deepening their faith and developing their leadership, while four are only providing activities for students, then the greater portion of conference resources should go to where disciples are being made. Measures of equality must be replaced with measures of effectiveness and difference.

When paradigms shift and everything goes back to zero, as mentioned earlier in chapter 3, everyone feels the discomfort that comes from unrequested changes. People quite rightly feel as if their contracts for membership in their local churches have been changed without their asking. Clergy feel quite rightly that their contracts for ordination have been changed without their asking. Bishops and district superintendents quite rightly feel that their contracts for leadership and supervision have been changed without their asking. It should come as no surprise that times of deep change are stressful and prompt strong actions and reactions among people. Suddenly an ordered world that once provided security becomes a wilderness requiring new learning and risk.

Reactions of people at such moments are predictable and familiar. Some will rush to defend the familiar, old practices by challenging leaders to follow the letter of the law or polity that came from the time of the earlier paradigm. Some will hunker down, feeling too old or inadequate to accommodate changes, hoping to be able to finish out their careers or membership before the change requires too much of them. Some, however, will align themselves with the change in outcomes and expend themselves missionally without guarantees of old rewards. Again, if the church would be a movement, then we need to recognize the reality that movements excite vision and require sacrifice but also engender resistance.

Connectionalism Reinvented

As systemic outcomes change, it is critical to remember that God is doing something with us and in our midst. The change we are experiencing can be much more than a retelling of an old institutional story with a new cultural or generational twist. Our hope, our testimony, is that this is God refining the organizational church for missional purpose. The new thing that is happening also challenges and changes our understanding and practice of connectionalism. Even here everything goes back to zero.

In the old paradigm, the outcome of the denominational system was institutional satisfaction. To that end clergy and congregations alike were invited to make *institutional* connections. In the new paradigm, we are now invited to make *missional* connections. Shared purpose and a common heart will keep us connected now.

"Who is my mother, who is my brother?" Mother, brother, disciples all must have surely felt that they understood their relationship to Jesus, relationships that gave them access to him and allowed them to trust what they could ask of him. Such relationships, especially those of mother and brother, are defined with clear expectations and obligations. A mother can expect to be obeyed, a brother listened to. Jesus, however, moves counter to all that is expected by challenging the issue of relationship. The mother or brother is the one who does the will of God. Connection was redefined not as familial relationship but as shared purpose.

The earliest connection of Methodism was similarly a connection of shared purpose and practice. If your heart is as my heart, said John Wesley, then give me your hand.[6] The connection was around shared purpose and common mission. From the perspective of purpose and mission, ordination is not by itself a definition of connection, because one can be ordained but not pursue the making of disciples. From the perspective of purpose and mission, payment of apportionments is not a definition of connection, because a congregation may be capable of paying its full apportionment without having any concern for the mission field.

Our confusion about connection in the present moment may be a special case of mis-application of covenant. Covenant is a basic form of belonging based on promise. Israel promised to be the people of God, and God promised to be the God of Israel. The promise was based on behavior. The people were to follow the precepts of God. Their behavior was measured with blessings and curses. When Israel was faithful to the precepts the people were blessed, and when unfaithful the people were cursed. When God was faithful with the people God was blessed, and when people felt God to be unfaithful, the boldest of the prophets would curse God. Indeed at the center of the story of Job is the anomaly of a man who refuses to curse God when God treated him unfairly.

Congregations and denominations use a similar set of blessings and curses to mark faithfulness or unfaithfulness. The dilemma in the current misunderstanding of covenant is that mainline denominations use *institutional* measures of faithfulness. In a memorable consultation with a congregation, I worked with leaders who wanted to explore the reasons and limits of their membership growth, which over the past five years averaged 4 percent (a steady and notable level of growth). Not long into the conversation I noted that the leaders were complaining about how their church was not growing. I pointed out the discrepancy between the data and their conversation. Yes, the leader conceded that the church was growing, "but," he continued (the proverbial "but" that negates the first part of any sentence), "they aren't good members." When pushed to describe a "good" member, this group described a person who attended worship regularly, provided regular financial support, provided leadership by getting involved in planning and committees, and was a regular participant in congregational groups and activities. This group of leaders was, in fact, describing themselves. Note, however, that each of these measures of "good" is an institutional measure of resources and activities, inputs and throughputs. People connected to this congregation were being either blessed or cursed. They were blessed by being called good members if they fulfilled the institutional expectations of others; they were identified as bad members if they did not match up with the expectations.

Congregations are likewise blessed or cursed as good or bad depending upon whether apportionments are paid, denominational priorities and programs followed, denominational curriculum used, and so forth. Bishops are blessed or cursed depending upon whether clergy and congregational expectations are met in appointments or whether the letter of the law is being followed. So, as noted in chapter 2, an earlier connection that was once based on shared theology and history came to be replaced by connection defined institutionally. The comparison used in chapter 2 is as follows.

The Initial Denominational Center	The Institutional Denominational Center
• Theology	• Appointments (clergy deployment)
• Polity	• Regulatory polity that manages competition by enforcing rules
• History	• Pension costs
• Location	• Health insurance
• Ethnicity	• Mission that goes beyond the capacity of the local church

Connection and covenant became misunderstood as blessings and curses around institutional matters and lead us to evaluate one another as good or bad.

Here again the paradigm shifts. Who is my mother, who is my brother? Which is the good person, the good clergy, the good congregation, the good bishop? It is he or she who willingly focuses on and holds himself or herself accountable to the mission—the changing of people into disciples who pursue personal piety and social holiness. As everything goes back to zero we become connected as United Methodists not by our past or by our institution but by our purpose. Extending the chart of the changing centers, I argue that we are now constructing a new definition of connection and connectionalism:

The Initial Denominational Center	The Institutional Denominational Center	The New Center of a Movement
· Theology	· Appointments (clergy deployment)	· Clear identity
· Polity	· Regulatory polity that manages competition by enforcing rules	· Common purpose
· History	· Pension costs	· Shared story that invites people of differences to connect to a shared center
· Location	· Health insurance	· Missional outcomes clearly described
· Ethnicity	· Mission that goes beyond the capacity of the local church	· Community as the gathering of the like-minded, not the like

In our search to become a movement, we are a people who are seeking connection through shared identity, purpose, and story that are directly aligned with our mission of changing people's lives through an encounter with Christ. We measure our connection by the shared difference we are trying to make, not by compliance to established institutional practices.

The good news is that such connectedness is not dependent upon agreement. Agreement (which is beyond the capacity of a large movement that stretches globally, spanning all orders of people, settings, and situations) is replaced by shared identity and purpose. This is one of the key lessons of our largest congregations that routinely bring together large gatherings of people who are amazingly diverse in age, race, theological perspective, political leanings, and personal preferences. Within mainline denominations people in such large congregations are not asked to resolve their differences by forced agreement with one another but are instead invited to become a community complete with differences. People become community by aligning themselves with the central story of the congregation and the outcomes that the church seeks to fulfill. It is not agreement that holds people together but shared identity (Who are we?) and shared purpose (What has God called us to do?).

Redefinition of connectionalism is a necessary step in the shift from consumer to citizen introduced earlier. When connected by institutional measures, we are consumers connected through the products and services offered by the denomination. We are connected through the compliance with the rules. Our blessings and curses are measures of whether denomination and people have met one another's expectations.

Movements require citizens, those willing to both serve and hold themselves accountable to the purpose of the whole church. Our connection depends upon whether we see ourselves linked in the same story and aligned with the same outcomes. Through our connection in Christ and the call to make disciples in a movement, it matters more what we accomplish than it matters how we accomplish it. There is ample room for diversity, differences, and disagreements if there is a shared center of story and purpose. Diversity, differences, and disagreements do not have to be resolved into agreement and sameness as a prerequisite to connection.

The work of creating and sustaining a movement is not legislative or regulatory. Movements are inherently messy since they gather together widely diverse people who share a common center. The only neatness in a movement comes from the clear outcomes and the clear identity that it invites a disparate people to share.

Having come so far since the 1960s when institutional red flags began to appear as warnings about a changed mission field, it is time to testify to what God is doing in us now. This is testimony in the sense of announcing God's activity as it is recognized. It is not a declaration of work completed; it is witness to change that has already begun. There is more yet to do, and what remains will be increasingly difficult.

Systems are built backwards. Returning to the system model of input—throughput—output, being able to clearly describe the intended output is the first but not the final step in building a system. It isn't until we are clear about our purpose that we have any idea about the resources needed or the activities required to produce desired results.

This is the dilemma in deep change in long-established institutions. Leaders who were initially called to be responsible for the rules, practices, and survival of the institution are the same leaders who are now called to redesign the system and realign resources and activities to accomplish new ends. Members, participants, and clergy who were invited to take the role of consumer are the same members, participants, and clergy now called to be citizens. This means acting against one's own self-interest in order to serve the greater mission. Looking ahead, the work will seem daunting. There may well be no happy way through the next steps. But if we allow, God's hand is clearly in the mix. While it may not yet be time to celebrate our metanoic, paradigmatic turnaround, it is time to testify.

CHAPTER FIVE

CITIZENSHIP IN THE MOVEMENT: VOTING AGAINST ONE'S SELF-INTEREST

Adopt the attitude that was in Christ Jesus:
Though he was in the form of God,
he did not consider being equal with God something to exploit.
But he emptied himself
by taking the form of a slave
and by becoming like human beings.

—Philippians 2:5-7

It was an ancient hymn, and quoting it to the Philippians might have been like a pastor today quoting "Amazing Grace" to a bunch of church-goers. Paul was using the familiar hymn to encourage others to think like Christ and to empty themselves.

Why do preachers quote a hymn, recite a poem, or tell a story? To underscore the point that they are already trying to make. So while this ancient but famous passage might stand alone for us as a statement of Jesus' nature as both human and divine (Christ's willingness to empty himself—*Kenosis*), for Paul it may well have been an intended underscoring of the main point that he wanted to make with his friends by encouraging them to have a mind like Christ's. Look at the verse that precedes the hymn, and the main point is uncovered: "Instead of each person watching out for their own good, watch out for what is better for others" (Philippians 2:4). To have the mind of Christ is to vote against one's own self-interest. It is an emptying of self in order to serve others.

Here lies one of the greatest challenges to our hope of reclaiming the energy and clarity of a newly expressed Wesleyan movement within our denominational institution. Institutions do not, particularly over time, lean away from but rather lean into self-interests. As noted earlier, Robert Quinn has rightly observed that established institutions are actually an aggregate of self-interest groups—subgroups that when gathered together make up a constituency of constituencies that form the structure of an institution. Each constituent subgroup quite naturally competes for attention, importance, and especially for resources. At a time when the future is unsure and resources seem scarce, constituencies awaken their self-interests and compete for security.

The current norm within the United Methodist denomination is to argue for one's interest. Clergy argue to protect practices of guaranteed appointments. Congregations argue for reduced apportionments. General and Jurisdictional Conference delegates are intentionally chosen so that a constituency's position on a contested issue will be represented to advantage. Committees and commissions on children's ministry argue the importance of their work and their need for staff and budget—as do committees and commissions on youth ministry, campus ministry, evangelism, stewardship, interfaith relations, ethnic ministries, camping, and the list goes on. The question is not if any or all of these efforts of ministry are "good," for certainly they are. What is at issue is that rather than community conversations about what is most "right" for a denomination in transition, the default mode is to increase energy and strategy to fight for resources to preserve or extend the interest of one's own constituent group.

It is increasingly common for me to be in conversation at any and all levels of the church where people openly acknowledge the unsustainability of the current denominational path. We can't keep doing what we are doing and live into a viable future, let alone have a ministry of fruitfulness in a changed mission field. This shared recognition has fueled efforts toward deep change.

It is equally common for me to be in gatherings at all levels of the church where initiatives of deep change are proposed and given enthusiastic support—until it comes time for implementation. In two very large conference gatherings in two separate conferences, a bishop stated plainly to the audience that moving into a proposed change would require the sacrifice of people voting against their own self-interest. In both cases the group responded with spontaneous applause indicating their agreement and willingness. We really do want change for our denomination. The steps into this conversation are very clear:

1. The recognition of our unsustainable current ways;

2. The push from leaders for deep change that goes beyond downsizing to save money or rearranging the organization to do the same work in some new way;

3. An energy and enthusiasm from followers to do what it takes to make us fruitful again, to return to our Wesleyan roots of movement;

However, to finish off the sequence, there is the fourth step that is also a part of the pattern. It is the step of natural resistance. The NIMBY (Not In My Back Yard) reaction when it comes to proposals of redirecting attention or resources. If there are priorities to be shifted, practices to be changed, a shift in the way resources are aligned for mission field outcomes, the normal response is that the church should find a way to do so without changing "my" own position or security in the organization, "my" funding or compensation, or the recognition of the importance of "my" own work and interests. If changes are to be made—Not In My Back Yard.

The response is a very normal and healthy reaction that seeks to retain what feels important to us and to protect what we are afraid we will lose. However, in order to reclaim ourselves with the vitality of a movement, we will need to work through this fourth step and move beyond it. In the midst of denominational turmoil it calls for a spiritual discipline from us. "Adopt the attitude that was in Christ Jesus: / Though he was in the form of God, / he did not consider being equal with God something to exploit. / But he emptied himself. . . ." Paul's point was: "Let each of you look not to your own interests, but to the interests of others."

What we are asked for is a conscious choice that comes from a discipline of faith. Do we choose to be consumer or citizen? Consuming is the posture of dependence, counting on the institution to protect and preserve what we do, what we individually believe, and where our greatest passions lie. To be a citizen in a movement is to respond to and take responsibility for the whole purpose of the church. Citizenship in the new Wesleyan movement requires us to join with others also committed to deep change that will reclaim our identity and purpose. It is to commit to deep change that will also change who we are, where we will fit into the organizational life of the denomination, where resources will be directed, and how decisions will be made.

Three Challenges of Citizenship in a New Wesleyan Movement

Of the many changes that we will need to address, there are three essential challenges that we, the clergy and the laity of the current United Methodist Church, will need to face in order to recapture the passion and focus of a movement that will make a spiritual difference in the new, changed mission field. We will need to break through the practices of institutional dependency that we have built. We will need to claim and accept our identity that unites us despite our differences. We will need to develop a trust that marks us as Christian community different from North American organizational norms.

Breaking Dependency

Ours is an institutional inheritance that has made us dependent on some other person or organizational body for responsibilities that actually must rest with us, as individuals. The clearest way to point to the dependence that we have nurtured is to consider the appointment process of our clergy to congregations. When a pastor receives an appointment that is not personally satisfying, difficult to the point of personal discomfort, or in some way a poor match of pastoral skills and congregational priorities, the question can be asked, whose problem is it? The short answer in a dependent system is that it is the district superintendent's problem. The pastor has the right to call the district superintendent and ask to be placed in a better, more appropriate, or more satisfying appointment in the next appointment cycle.

Similarly, when a congregation receives the appointment of a pastor who is not well liked, does not satisfy the expectations of the current members, or pushes for goals and programs that feel unsuited to the way the congregation has done things in the past, the question can be asked, whose problem is it? Again, the short answer in a dependent system is that it is the district superintendent's problem, and the Pastor Parish Relations Committee has the right to call the district superintendent and ask for a better, more appropriate, or more satisfying clergy appointment in the next appointment cycle.

In a dependent system the individual does not need to take responsibility for himself or herself but can put the responsibility on someone else to make something right. Such dependence in our denomination is one of the reasons that, despite years of acknowledging the importance of long-tenured clergy for the health and vitality of ministry in a congregation, the average tenure of clergy is still only a little over four years. Consider what might happen if clergy felt responsible to make their appointed congregations the right places for them to be in ministry by committing to negotiating with leaders through the tough stages of the pastoral relationship. Consider what it would be like if Pastor Parish Relations Committees felt responsible to work closely with their appointed pastor to negotiate the natural and necessary tensions that develop whenever a leader moves an organization toward its stated goals rather than simply telling the pastor to correct the complaints being heard about him or her.

At times of deep change it is difficult to move ahead. Each part of a dependent system waits for some other part to make things right or better. Clergy and congregations point to the conference and national church, assured that once that part of the church gets its act together, the congregation will be able to be more effective in ministry. While this congregational waiting is going on, the conference and national church focus on making local churches more effective, assuming that the change has to happen at the local level and once the change is underway the regional and national levels of the church will know what is needed to help. This dependence, which waits on some other part of the denominational system to make the required changes, leads to interesting expectations. Congregations expect annual conferences to cut their budgets to ease the burden on the local church while simultaneously expecting that no programs of importance to them will be cut, subsidies to struggling congregations will continue, and conference staff will be continually available to resource them. Similarly it leads to curious reactions in which the regional and national church insists on more reports in an effort to hold congregations accountable with the assumption that requiring additional reports is a service or resource for doing ministry.

Addressing the barrier of dependence in order to be a Wesleyan movement will require us to bridge the gap between what we say and how we behave. We speak of being missional in this moment to this changed culture. If we want to address the crisis of relevancy, in which our denomination has lost its ability to speak with a changed culture and with new generations, we need to align our resources, our attention, and our prayers with those efforts that best connect us to this culture in this moment. We cannot speak of addressing this new mission field and continue to work from old, established budgets that still reflect old commitments (as noble and good as they may be) to practices and programs that do not move us toward our outcome. Old commitments may still be important and valuable, but they cannot be resourced at the same levels.

We need to be inventive to be faithful in our commitments while directing resources, attention, and prayer to the issues that rest at the heart of the movement of introducing personal and social holiness by making disciples. We cannot ask our local congregations to be bold in claiming their mission and mission field, then link them together in a two- or three-point charge for the purpose of providing a single salary and benefit package for a full-time pastor. In doing so we ask the church to be intentionally missional and then tell the church that its real mission is to supply compensation for its pastor. We cannot restructure our conferences to be nimble and responsive to the mission field using old technologies that don't connect us to new generations, insisting that no staff changes be made, no subsidies cut, or no committees go unbudgeted. Moving from consumer to citizen requires us to move away from dependence on the denomination for our security and to step up to inventiveness and risk that address the whole of the purpose of our denomination in a changed mission field.

Breaking dependence will require our willingness to seek and accept real measures for our ministry. The issue of measures has prompted very difficult conversations over past years. Clergy are generally resistant to their congregations being measured (number of members, average attendance, number of confessions of faith, baptisms) because such measures do not reflect changes in the generational behaviors of people and are as driven by community demographics as by the efforts of the pastor or congregation. On the other side, denominational leaders press for measures, well aware that our current measures are inadequate but also knowing that a system gets what it measures. (A system that measures nothing gets what it measures.) In a dependent system in which clergy and congregations are consumers of the care and attention of the denomination, measures are threatening because measuring results challenges dependence and assumes responsibility. Fruitfulness, being known by one's fruit, is built on the idea that we are to make a difference. Something is to be intentionally changed because of our encounter with Christ. Following Christ calls for a response that changes us and is meant to change the world. Consumers attend to their own needs, but citizens focus on the needs of the person that they have been called to become and on the needs of the world in which they have been placed.

The question for the United Methodist denomination is no longer whether our ministry should be measured but whether we are willing to learn how to measure our ministry without being stymied by the limits of quantitative measures. The critical hint comes from Jim Collins in his work on nonprofit organizations, all of which are challenged by the difficulty of quantitative measures of the changes that they seek to make. How does one measure a changed person? Collins points out that when one can't quantify results by counting the difference to be measured, then one has to be willing to describe the difference.[1] At every level of the system leaders need to describe the difference they are trying to make with the greatest detail they can muster. Only then can we have conversations in our congregations, our conferences, and our national agencies about whether there is evidence that we are moving toward the change that we want. If quantifying the results of our ministry is the science of leadership, then describing the results we are called to make and measuring our fruitfulness by intentional and disciplined conversation is the art of leadership. A movement must be intentional and focused on change. The original Wesleyan movement set about to change people and to spread scriptural holiness throughout the land. Wesley had clear conversations with circuit riders about their effectiveness. The agendas of early Methodist conferences focused on whether the desired change was being addressed. Breaking dependence requires a willingness to return to old practices of measured conversations about describable fruits.

If breaking dependence involves a willingness to be measured, the concomitant necessity is a willingness to be supervised. In his study of educational systems, Tony Wagner notes that, as a professional group, teachers prefer to work alone rather than as part of a team. The teacher's classroom is his or her personal domain, and when the principal steps in to do the required supervision, the visit is treated as an intrusion.[2] A similar observation can be made about clergy who perform their leadership in the discrete setting of their local churches. Supervisory visits by district superintendents or supervisory reporting to bishops are also seen as unwanted intrusions by folks who don't understand the local situation or who have nothing to bring to the conversation. What is lost in both the classroom and the congregation is reflective dialogue between people who have a shared investment in the work and who have the capacity to help one another learn their way into new challenges.

Evaluation is a feared topic among clergy and congregations despite the fact that a quiet and low-grade evaluation is commonly the undercurrent of conversations about whether a church "likes" its pastor or a pastor "likes" his or her appointment. Any formal evaluation is feared because it brings with it a sense of judgment. It is a known truism that no church wants to evaluate its pastor and no conference wants to evaluate its bishop, unless the people are already dissatisfied with their leader. The sense of judgment is already present, and the process of evaluation is used as the tool to bring the judgment to conclusion.

Supervision and evaluation are very different practices. Supervision, done well, is not a judgment but a conversation about moving toward a described difference. As such, supervision depends upon intent. One needs to identify and claim what is intended to be different because of one's being or work. In chapter 3, I spoke of publicing—the practice of making one's intent known.

A favorite story of mine is about a friend who gave himself a fortieth birthday gift of tap dancing lessons. He had long wanted to learn to tap dance and, at forty, thought that dancing would benefit both his health and his agility. So off he went to his first class, where he was the only male in a class of females—all under thirteen years old. His first reaction was to quit the class. But he decided that he really did want to know how to dance, and it really would make him feel better. That evening he wrote invitations to his closest friends to attend the recital at the end of his lessons. He stated his intent with his friends. He publiced. In return he received continual support and accountability. Every time he saw one of his friends he was asked about his dancing. He never remembered a time in which he felt so accountable to finish something, and he never experienced so much support and interest from all of those friends who were watching him. Publicing, the statement of intent to those who will walk alongside, invites and structures supervision, which is a conversation of accountability and support.

To break our institutional dependence we need to both seek and submit to supervision. The act of naming an intent (we will increase the number of adult confessions of faith this year; we will elect people to our board who will themselves practice disciplines of faith as an act of leadership) is an act of responsibility. We willingly risk naming what we intend to do even when not sure of the results, rather than make no claim for a difference we feel called to make. To not risk claiming an intent is to remain dependent on the system to tell us what to do.

Bishops need to public the intended change that they want for their conference with their fellow/sister bishops in their Colleges and Council. Clergy need to public the intended change that they feel called to bring to their congregation with their district superintendent, their clergy peers, and their church leaders. Church leaders need to public their intended change with their members and district superintendent. Without intents—clear, specific descriptions of the difference we believe we are called to make—there will be no supervisory conversations of accountability and support. There will be no questions of: how it is going? What are you learning? What are you going to try next? What resources are you using? Without supervision there is just waiting to be told what to do and the continued trying of what we've already done.

Claiming Our Identity

The second challenge of citizenship in a new Wesleyan movement will be our willingness to claim a shared identity. This may not be personally comfortable, but it is essential to our purpose.Return to Quinn's observation that, over time, established institutions develop both a public mission (which they announce to the world) and a private mission (in which they quietly pursue the satisfaction of the strongest constituent voices in the institution).[3] The private mission of serving the internal constituents of the institution is the silent but more powerful of the two missions.

With both a public and a private mission it is also common for those who are a part of the institution to have both a public and a private identity. In The United Methodist Church our shared and public identity is as a people who make disciples. We are a people of a practical theology who are called to both change the lives of individuals through disciple making and change the world through disciples. However, because of our size, geography, diversity, and multiple historic denominational origins those in The United Methodist Church with a shared public identity can also hold private constituent identities as subgroups within the whole.

In fact, within The United Methodist Church I would argue that many of us have either a constituent subgroup identity, a positional subgroup identity, or both. A constituent identity is one in which we share with others the passion or importance of a particular component part of mission or ministry. The United Methodist denomination holds many such constituent subgroups that come with rich histories and records of accomplishment. Consider groups such as United Methodist Women, Volunteers in Mission, United Methodist Campus Ministry Association, Black United Methodists for Church Renewal, Methodist Federation for Social Action, The Fellowship of United Methodists in Music and Worship Arts, and The Hispanic Plan. Anyone familiar with a mainline denomination knows that such a list of subgroups can go on at great length. Usually organized at a regional or national level, these groups also have adherents in local churches, where the importance of their agendas is made known. The advantage and value of such groups is that they provide both energy and strategies to do ministry in a multitude of ways to address a multitude of needs. However, in a time of deep change requiring new alignment of resources, these subgroups invite us to compete over resources. As resources are stretched and diminished, the competition among subgroups becomes more fierce. The mission of the whole may not thrive because of the passion of the parts. Citizenship does not ask us to relinquish our passions and commitments. Passions can continue with new plans and creative strategies that are less resource dependent. But citizenship in the movement does ask us to serve the public mission first and to align our private passions with the shared public mission.

Different from constituent identities are the positional identities that develop in our denomination based on a conclusion that we have reached and feel compelled to defend. A positional subgroup is one in which we share a theological position or belief with others. Such a positional identity comes from a conviction of a truth that we hold in contrast to those of opposing positions whose truth we find to be false. Competing spiritual truths have lived in tension throughout the history of the church. In fact, Nancey Murphy tracks from our earliest Christian origin some of the contentious philosophical differences that now divide us on issues such as abortion and homosexuality, suggesting that they are not resolvable.[4]

Positional subgroups may be either denominational or ecumenical, with different levels of formal organization, but their names are well known: The Confessing Movement, Affirmation, Reconciling Ministry Network, Good News, The Institute for Religion and Democracy, Church within a Church. Again, these are passionate people who find their faith galvanized by personal experience. The advantage and value of such groups is that together they can help us find the truths and values that lie on opposing sides of difficult issues. However, positions (conclusions) are notoriously nonnegotiable. One of the fundamental lessons of conflict management is that once a position is claimed there is no negotiation because any negotiated agreement changes the position, which then, by definition, is not the accepted position. If constituent identities invite us to compete for resources, positional identities invite us to break relationships. Citizenship in a Wesleyan movement does not ask us to give up our claims for truth or our understanding of God's claim in our own life. But citizenship does ask us to live uncomfortably with those of other positions who share with us a public identity of purpose and mission.

While it may seem difficult to think of living in a shared identity with those who hold opposing positions, I find I am helped by thinking in terms of distance rather than agreement. Martin Marty pointed to philosopher Arthur Schopenhauer's discussion of civil association that included a story of a colony of porcupines:

There was once a colony of porcupines. They were wont to huddle together on a cold winter's day and, thus wrapped in communal warmth, escape
from being frozen. But, plagued with the pricks of each other's quills,
they drew apart. And every time the desire for warmth brought them
together again, the same calamity overtook them. Thus they remained,
distracted between two misfortunes, able neither to tolerate nor to do
without each other, until they discovered that when they stood at a certain
distance from one another they could both delight in one another's indi-
viduality and enjoy one another's company. They did not attribute any
metaphysical significance to this distance, nor did they image it to be an
independent source of happiness, like finding a friend. They recognized
it to be a relationship in terms not of substantive enjoyments but of con-
tingent considerabilities that they must determine for themselves.
Unknown to themselves they had invented civil association.[5]

I would claim that Schopenhauer was describing, more than civil association, authentic community, indeed, authentic Christian community.
Once any family, group, or community intentionally moves beyond the ini-
tial politeness of false community where we claim agreement, discomfort
ensues. But where there is strong purpose discomfort, even to the point of
deep disagreement, asks us not to castigate or revile one another but to find
an appropriate distance that will keep us connected in purpose without
unduly pricking one another. Movements have been historically and notoriously fraught with different and competing agendas of the individuals and
groups who make up the movement. But participation in the movement is
still of high value because its purpose is larger and more demanding than
agreement about constituent or positional identities. To return to a
Wesleyan movement requires us to vote against our self-interests, even our
self-truths, and claim the larger purpose we hold as a people of a practical
theology who believe that following Christ continually changes us and
transforms the world.

Developing Trust

The third of the challenges of citizenship in a Wesleyan movement is
the risk of trust. In a dependent system where people wait for others to
serve their needs and solve their problems, any move by someone in
authority is suspect because decisions made may or may not meet the need
of the dependent individual. Trust is given only to those who make deci-

sions in one's favor, and even that trust is not extended to future decisions. Dependent systems do not run on trust. Everything must be vetted by all.

As a consultant to congregations for thirty years, I have been continually surprised and dismayed while doing the work of conflict management. I was always prepared for people not to trust me as the third party stranger to their conversation. People in conflict don't turn to a consultant without some level of hope that the consultant will take their side, so there is always a period of distrust until folks see how the consultant operates. Trust was for me to earn, not assume.

I was not, however, prepared for the mistrust that people in Christian community hold for one another. If a layperson did not agree with the pastor, I was told that he or she was a resister trying to undermine the pastor's leadership. If a district superintendent was involved, I was told he or she was there only as a representative of the clergy union and would automatically take the pastor's side. If the pastor was displeased with his or her appointment, I was told that that bishop made the appointment as a punishment to the pastor, to the congregation, or both. If the conference evidenced concern about the conflict, I was told it was only because they were worried about apportionments.

Of course this is natural. Whenever a system is in distress and doesn't know what went wrong, it wants to know who went wrong. We easily slide into the temptation of blaming. Nonetheless, I have consistently found it painful to see how quickly people in the church ascribe negative motives to one another before listening to one another. I suspect I might not have been so surprised had I been quicker to put my experience into a biblical perspective. Every time Jesus invited those of high stature to step down and those of humble state to step up, there were those who wondered what he got out of it. They judged his motives either militaristic or blasphemous. Paul's letters were an ongoing commentary of the competition of evangelists as reported by Chloe's people, squabbling among believers, and the contentiousness of those who challenged his credentials, thinking that he wanted control.

To reclaim ourselves as a Wesleyan movement will require trust, which means relinquishing a part of ourselves to the other to whom we give our trust. I suspect that the importance of trust in a spiritual movement is self-evident. Nonetheless, I point to two critical reasons that demand trust.

The first is the more modest and strategic reason. The crisis of relevance announced in our denomination rests on our inability to talk with the changed culture in our new technological, generational, and global mission field. One of the hallmarks of this changed culture is speed— instantaneous communication and information; technological leap-frogging where the next generation of phone or computer is released before the problems of the present generation are fixed; people who work in teams or task groups rather than committees; and so on. Part of our deep desire to be a movement is to be nimble in order to live in this new world. We want to trade rules and regulations for purpose and principles so that we can address future ministry without being constrained by residual history. Organizational speed depends upon trust. Speed, agility, responsiveness, which are the currency of this culture, cannot be embedded in an organization that lacks trust and insists that every decision be weighed, explained, and vetted with multiple groups in order to move ahead.

Measures of ministry, supervision, and accountability are not tools of mistrust. Practiced well, these are the ways in which we continually remind ourselves what we are about and what is of greatest missional importance. These are the ways in which we have conversations about moving quickly ahead without stopping for permission or agreement at every step.

If speed is the lesser reason for trust, disciple making is the greater reason. Trust is a discipline of faith. Trust is not natural to people biological-ly and emotionally hard-wired for survival. Offering trust is a discipline, not a natural reaction. It is also a great risk because the trust may not be returned. One of the most difficult realities in a family, marriage, or friendship when trust is broken is that the only way to rebuild it is to give it. We can't demand trust from others. We can only give it ourselves.

If we are to make disciples, is this not a discipline that we want not only to teach but more importantly to practice? Disciplines are actions. Trust involves the action of intentionally ascribing the best, not the worst, motives to the actions of others. Trust involves the action of listening, by which we try to truly understand the other, not just to figure out what to say next to win our advantage.

If there are personal disciplines of trust, there are also communal forms. When we submit our personal agenda to it, holy conferencing is an act of trust that God's Spirit can move in a group. Bishop Sally Dyck has been a leader in inviting us to learn to practice this discipline. Working with a group of leaders from across the United States, she has helped shape practices that can help us to holy conference rather than to meet in civic dispute.[6] Emphasizing listening over talking, being willing to consider that I might be wrong, intentionally inviting the Holy Spirit into the conversation, and framing questions in terms of the greater or common good instead of self-interest are all part of a list of behaviors in which I practice holy conferencing and risk trust.

Ours is a church that would be a movement. We cannot dismantle our institutional side because we do, in fact, need some form of infrastructure to organize and align us. But if enough of us shift from consumer to citizen and from self-interest to missional purpose, we have the capacity to birth a movement within our institutional self. It is to this building of a movement inside of an institution that we turn next.

CHAPTER SIX

CAN DAVID LIVE
WITH GOLIATH? CAN
A MOVEMENT LIVE INSIDE
AN INSTITUTION?

A champion named Goliath from Gath came out from the Philistine camp. He was more than nine feet tall. He had a bronze helmet on his head and wore bronze-scale armor weighing one hundred twenty-five pounds. He had bronze plates on his shins, and a bronze scimitar hung on his back. His spear shaft was as strong as the bar on a weaver's loom, and its iron head weighed fifteen pounds. His shield-bearer walked in front of him.

—1 Samuel 17:4-7

In preparation for battle Saul clothed David with his armor in the same fashion as Goliath, and the result was that David "tried in vain to walk." It was too much and too heavy. David chose instead to go into battle lightly—a staff in his hand, five smooth stones, and a sling. Agility prevailed over size. Inventiveness and risk defeated strength. Quick and agile movement easily bested slow and cumbersome institution.

This chapter will raise the question of whether Goliath and David can live together. There are those who want to live fully within the institutional denomination with its weight, orderly strategies, and defenses, while others want to travel lightly as a movement, able to move freely and quickly, unhampered by custom, tradition, or law. Can the United Methodist denomination be a large and orderly global institution, yet be a spiritual renewal movement?

Institutions and movements do not live comfortably with one another, but they do not need to be framed as incompatible opposites. Institutions and movements can be understood as equal truths that can inform each other, even if they cannot be held simultaneously. We do, however, need to break through the argument of how the church is to be dressed for battle. Do we need to cling closely to the weight of full dress with denominational orderly divisions, agencies, conferences, districts, rules, laws, and norms of practice? Do we move quickly and lightly as a movement, putting on only the whole armor of God—the simple belt of truth, the breastplate of righteousness, the shield of faith, the helmet of salvation, and the sword of the Spirit? (See Ephesians 6:14-17.) Or are there roles for both Goliath and David, structure and freedom, weight and agility?

It is not likely that The United Methodist Church will fully and only become a Wesleyan movement, turning its back on institutional steadiness in favor of passion and inventiveness. There are aspects of an institution that are of high value that we cannot lose. There is a need for an orderly structure upon which a fully global church must live and function, communicating clearly, directing resources with some effectiveness, and mounting efforts of health, wholeness, and social justice. These essentials are beyond the capacities of smaller and less coordinated portions of the denominational body.

Wisdom suggests that it is not wise to put denomination and movement against one another as contestants in the church, with winners and losers, right and wrong. The United Methodist Church is a denomination and needs to continue. The United Methodist Church is seeking also to be a Wesleyan movement of renewal, both to the individual and to the denomination itself. Rather than ask the question of how does one turn a global and structured institution into a movement, the better question may be to ask what does a global and structured institution want from a movement? What is missing that would be of value? What is possible that needs to be considered?

What Do We Want from a Movement?

A Presbyterian executive friend suggested a book to me several years ago that he found helpful but couldn't quite explain why. The book was Ori Brafman and Rod Beckstrom's *The Starfish and the Spider: The Unstoppable Power of*

Leaderless Organizations.[1] Brafman and Beckstrom's book compared hierarchical, centralized organizations (spiders) and flat, decentralized organizations (starfish). Centralized organizations, while stable and predictable, are characteristically slow and regulated, depending upon clear hierarchical structure in which authority comes from "the top." Like a spider, if the head is cut off, the organization dies. Starfish (decentralized, "leaderless" organizations), on the other hand, are much more agile and malleable. If one part is cut off from the rest, the severed part will regenerate and continue on. Without being able to put his finger on it, my friend recognized that the tension between the starfish and the spider was at the heart of his Presbyterian (and our United Methodist) dilemma.

The difference between centralized and decentralized organizations has been recognized for a long time. I have used the difference between spiders and starfish while working with a good number of United Methodist leaders in a number of groups and have experienced consistent interest and energy in applying the ideas to the current denominational conversation. The United Methodist denomination currently is structured and practices its denominational life as a spider that wants (at least in part) to be a starfish. However, as we will see later, spiders that are troubled by their constraints struggle to become starfish only to discover, when successful, that they eventually become troubled by their lack of organization and want to become spiders again. Organizations and institutions routinely live their lives on a pendulum swinging from centralized to decentralized poles, seeking to capture the strength missing when operating too close to one pole or the other. Having spent a good deal of time as a spider, the mainline church now seeks the starfish. There is a wish for, instead of Goliath's armor, the quickness and freedom of a simple sling with stones. Knowing that perfection does not rest at either extreme, what does the institutional United Methodist denomination want from the possibility of a Wesleyan movement? I would suggest that there are four primary hopes in those who seek a reform movement in the church.

A Central and Sustained Attention to Mission and Purpose

In my last book, *Journey in the Wilderness*, I described our wandering in the wilderness. Since the mid-1960s the mainline church has explored church

71

growth, congregational transformation, and mandatory leadership development as avenues to address the decline of membership and importance of the church in American culture.[2] My conclusion was that each of these explorations was valuable and a source of new insight to help congregations live in the new American reality. However, rather than "fixing" the church or solving the dilemma of reaching out to new generations, the three earlier paths in the wilderness actually lead to a fourth path and a better question, of purpose and outcomes. At its best the mainline church has learned that, above institutional survival and more than organizational neatness and compliance, what matters is mission and purpose—the why of ministry rather than the how or what. The question that is most important for congregations and denominations to answer is the question of call, of purpose. Rather than ask how we get more members or more dollars to sustain the life of the congregation, we need leaders to ask what difference they are called to make in the corner of God's kingdom where they are placed. Rather than ask how a conference increases apportionment giving or subsidizes struggling congregations, we need leaders to ask what their mission field looks like and what is the best way to use the church's resources (spiritual, human, financial, and facility resources) to offer the hope of Christ and introduce the possibility of difference.

Can we make first things first in the church? An observation of Brafman and Beckstrom is that, in starfish organizations, what lies at the center and serves as "the glue that holds decentralized organizations together" is ideology.[3] What the church wants from movement is to be held together by what we believe and what we are called to do because of our faith. There is a myriad of institutional issues that must be addressed and cannot be sidestepped. Nonetheless, it is not our collection or inheritance of problems that holds us together at the center but rather our purpose. Movements pay attention to purpose and outcomes while institutions can easily be distracted by problems and needs. Denominations seem to be captured by the hows and whats of institutionalism. Returning to the core ideology seems possible through a Wesleyan movement.

In chapter 4, we looked at a system through the Deming lens in which the component parts of input, throughput, and output offered clarity to distinguish between resources, activities, and outcomes. One of the deep difficulties of nonprofit organizations like churches and denominations was identified as the lack of understanding outcomes. One of the other deep difficulties of organizational systems is the inability to identify and focus on what Deming called the "core process," the simplest transaction of the system between inputs and outputs.[4] Effective leaders must be able to identify the difference their organization or institution is called to make, then also be able to identify and focus on the most essential activities of the organization, the core process, that will best accomplish the outcome.

Using the example of a woolen shirt as an output of a system, the input would be sheep. With sheep as the input and a woolen shirt as the output, the core process (the simplest, most direct throughput) is a rather simple series of activities. The person making the woolen shirt must know how to shear the sheep, card and weave the wool into cloth, then cut and sew the cloth into a shirt. Shearing, carding, weaving, cutting, and sewing are the activities that form the core process—the simplest transaction that can get from the input of sheep to the output of shirt. If these activities are not kept central and done well, a quality woolen shirt is not possible.

While that all seems rather simple and direct the reality is that, once a person moves from making a single woolen shirt to manufacturing woolen shirts the complexity of the endeavor overwhelms. Attention is distracted from the core purpose, eventually minimizing its importance. Different from a person who makes a single woolen shirt, leaders of a company that manufactures woolen shirts are required also to give attention to facilities, equipment, employees, hiring and firing practices and a host of human resource regulations, insurance, marketing, storage, transportation of goods, customer relations, OSHA standards, and risk management, all of which make up only a portion of the issues and problems that a manufacturing organization must be able to face. Over time the attention of leaders is drawn away from the core process of the organization and even drawn away from the final output of the woolen shirt, which often accounts for the lack of quality of the product produced. The core process and the output are outranked by the immediate organizational or institutional problems that come to the fore seeking the attention of leaders. Whether we are talking about manufacturing companies, banks and financial institutions, professional basketball teams, or mainline denominations, once distractions accumulate and create a crisis, the natural and appropriate reaction is to go back to basics. The United Methodist Church is seeking to go back to basics and is seeking a movement within itself to recapture the basics of identity, purpose, and call.

A Way to Cut through the "No's"

Those who are seeking a return to a sense of movement within the denominational church are also seeking a way to move efforts and initiatives ahead without having to negotiate a maze of hurdles and boundaries that have the capacity to defeat the effort toward the purpose of the church. Leaders are seeking ways to escape the gauntlet of "no's". Several years ago I was invited to do an organizational and staffing assessment of an annual conference for which I conducted a series of interviews, as well as considered an array of documents, reports, and data. In the interviews I asked staff and conference leaders how they would proceed in their conference if they had a new idea. The responses prompted the following portion of the report:

> A system with the power of 'no': Without a clear decision making system in the conference with the authority to make choices there is no clear path ahead around which strategies can be built and resources can be directed to make a desired difference. The fallback position in such systems is to force leaders to negotiate change by networking. Leaders, not given the authority to make clear decisions, need to negotiate support for their proposals. Forward movement can be stopped by any group or person who has the power to say no. When asked how a significant new idea could move ahead in the conference the persons interviewed identified 7 levels or gates that an idea would have to pass through before it could live:
>   Take it to the bishop to see if he agrees; and from there it needs to
>   Be taken to the appointment cabinet to see if they think they can do it;
>   Be taken to the extended cabinet to see if they think they can do it;
>   Be taken to the Vision Team to see if it violates the intent of the conference commitments;
>   Be taken to the *Book of Discipline* to see if it conforms to polity;
>   Be taken to Council on Finance and Administration to see if we can afford it; and finally

Be taken to [the large representational clergy and lay leadership group]
to see if we can "sell it" broadly enough to get support.

Significantly each of the seven levels identified in this decision-
making network has the capacity to defeat the new idea simply by saying no.

In contrast with such institutional gate keeping and the requirement to
negotiate a way through the maze of representational interests, those who
see the possibility of a movement within the institution are seeking the freedom to make decisions based on call and purpose. Those seeking a movement are also looking for a means by which decisions can be made at the
"local" level (whether that be at the congregational, district, or conference
level) rather than having to seek permission from a "higher court." It is an
effort to reclaim the work of ministry closest to the level where people actually do the ministry of disciple making. If a starfish organization is a helpful way to think about a movement, what is being sought here is what
Brafman and Beckstrom refer to as an "open system." In an open system
"everyone is entitled to make his / her own decisions and there are rules and
norms but these aren't enforced by anyone."[5] They go on to say that open
systems focus on the participants, not the leaders. "In an open system, what
matters most isn't the CEO but whether the leadership is trusting enough
of members to leave them alone."[6]

Being left alone and being trusted is not the same as an absence of
accountability. There are, of course, and always will be those who prefer not
to have to seek permission for or be held accountable for their performance
toward the outcomes of their organization. For some the absence of
accountability allows the absence of performance. Nonetheless, the search
for ways to develop a movement is for most people an effort not to escape
accountability but rather to enable decisions to be made by people at levels
where the ministry of the church is done.

It was instructive for me to listen to the language of a young (under
thirty-five years old) clergyperson at one of our Texas Methodist
Foundation learning gatherings in Austin. This young man wanted to be a
part of the United Methodist denomination but did not necessarily want to
be appointed to a local congregation under the authority of the bishop and
the *Book of Discipline*. He was actively engaged in ministry as a United
Methodist, and clearly he wanted to be United Methodist because of the

history and theology of the denomination. He had been invited to our learning gathering because of the excellence of his leadership and the remarkable effectiveness of the ministry of the group he led. "I needed a tether to an organization that supported me but did not constrain me," he said. He was not seeking freedom from discipline and accountability. He was doing ministry with a group of people who were not institutionally oriented but were actively seeking Christ in their lives and resonated strongly with the Methodist commitment to personal piety and social holiness.

Tethered is not a word commonly used in our connectional church, which typically thinks instead of commitments and requirements. The looser feel of the word *tethered* rather than *tied* gives expression to a desire to be a part of the United Methodist body without being subjected to institutional requirements and seven levels of no. It is not yet clear what form the connection should be within an institutional church that wants to form its covenant around identity and purpose rather than around institutional requirements. However, the attractiveness of being a movement may well be the language we are using to have this conversation about being connected without being constrained. While institutions rely upon regulations, movements thrive on principles and trust.

Equality at the Table

Movements are less hierarchical than institutions. Movements have leaders and followers. Institutions and bureaucracies have multiple levels of redundant decision making and reporting. In his review of the development of new forms of congregations such as the emerging and the emergent churches, Eddie Gibbs makes the observation that "hierarchical structures are increasingly problematic because decision making has to go through a chain of command and levels of control. . . . Vertical relationships are emphasized at the expense of horizontal engagement."[7] He later observes, "a growing number of churches are moving from a centralized approach to a more network-oriented approach involving clusters or mid-sized communities, in order to develop an ever-increasing number of neighborhood faith communities."[8] The shift from a vertical, organizational alignment to a horizontal (network), missional alignment is also part of what the denomination wants as it explores a part of its life as a movement.

In a network organization all of those who come to the table are equals. "Once you join," note Brafman and Beckstrom in their description of starfish organizations, "you're an equal."[9] The organizational form of a network is a circle, and they further note that because circles don't have hierarchies or structure, they are not guided by rules because no one has the power to enforce rules in a circle of equals. Healthy network circles do, however, have norms and purpose that become the foundation on which the circle rests. Norms and purpose work within a circle organization because of the realization that if individuals at the table do not follow the norms and focus on the purpose no one else will either. Network organizations, circles, and movements are self-organizing and self-regulating. "Members enforce the norms with one another."[10]

Perhaps even more powerful than the organizational effectiveness of a circle is the theology of the circle described by Tom Porter in his work on transformational conflict.

> Sitting in circle expresses in a physical and symbolic way the interconnectedness, interdependence, and unity of all life as found in God, with deep appreciation for diversity and the unique wisdom and contribution of each person. Everyone in the circle is the alpha and omega of the circle, with equal responsibility and accountability for the work of the circle.
>
> The circle emphasizes collective and communal wisdom and discernment. We are all on the same side of the table. The circle becomes a place to practice the Great Commandment, which is the sum of the law and the prophets: loving God, neighbor, and self. It is all about relationships, the healing of relationships and the formation of the community. The circle symbolizes and establishes the community we want to be. My understanding is the circle is the strongest shape in creation, stronger than anything that has corners. The circle can become a spiral as the circle moves deeper and deeper.[11]

Equality at the table and the power of the circle, where each participant holds equal responsibility and accountability, is highly attractive to a people who want to see their denominational institution behave more like a Wesleyan movement.

Catalysts and Champions

In their work on spider and starfish organizations, Brafman and Beckstrom identify the roles of catalysts and champions. A catalyst is, in chemistry, any element or compound that initiates a reaction without fusing into that reaction. Organizationally these are people who get a decentralized organization going and then cede control directly to the members without getting in the way.[12] Champions are relentless in promoting new ideas, behaving more like salespeople than like organizers or connectors.[13] Catalysts and champions are not roles commonly represented in institutions and democracies, but they are roles highly praised in movements. The fourth hope of what the denomination is seeking in reclaiming movement is catalytic and champion leadership.

Institutional Roles

For more than six years, I have served as a facilitator for gatherings of bishops and district superintendents as well as served in a coaching relationship with bishops, district superintendents, and Directors of Connectional Ministries. I have also worked with a number of extended cabinets as they have pursued their own work as conference leaders. In each of these settings a dominant theme has been an examination of their role and what is needed from them for conference leadership. The traditional institutional and inherited roles of these people have centered on management: regulation, service provision, and problem solving.

Management

Mainline denominations, including The United Methodist Church, have been recognized as managerial organizations dependent upon standard practices that are based on established norms and regulations and dependent upon certification processes for leaders that establish uniformity of expectation and accountability. In fact, deviation from standardized practices of management is constrained even in times of change, when leadership is needed.[14] The primary roles traditionally expected from our leaders are the management of the system and making sure that things are done right—even when doing things "right" has been proved to be ineffective or counterproductive.

78

Regulation

Closely tied to management is the role of regulator. As seen earlier, a connectionalism originally based on theology and mission was later replaced with a connectionalism based on a host of institutional measures such as compliance with polity, appointments, apportionments, pensions, and benefits. With such institutional measures at the center, the mainline denominations created a growing need for leaders who would regulate compliance to institutional connections. Orderliness and cohesion were managed by being sure that congregations, clergy, and other people and parts of the system adhered to rules and standard practice, even when inventiveness and agility were desired. The traditional understanding of leadership in such a system is as a follower, interpreter, and enforcer of the rules, norms, and standard practices.

Service Provision

Part of the argument of this book is that the recent stage of mainline denominational life in the United States has fostered an unhelpful and unhealthy dependence between members, clergy, congregations, and their denomination. If leaders in the congregation were not sure what to do, conference leaders were to provide training. If conference leaders were not sure what to do, general agency leaders were to provide training. If congregations needed new clergy leaders, conference leaders were to provide the rightly discerned candidate for appointment. If literature for Christian discipleship and learning were needed, the denominational publishing house was to provide curriculum. Much of the role of the denominational leader, at all levels of the denomination, from local church to general board, was to discern or research the need of some other part of the system and then meet that need with products or services.

Problem Solving

Closely tied to each of the above roles is the foundational role of problem solver in a dependent denominational system. Don't have the right clergy person appointed to your church? Take your problem to your district super-intendent and bishop. Don't have a strong connection to your community as a congregation? Take your problem to the Director of Connectional Ministries and get some demographic resources and training for how to understand the community. Can't afford to catch up with your deferred maintenance on your facilities? Take your problem to your Foundation and ask about options for applying for grants or reduced loan payments. As you would imagine, the list goes on at some length, and each level of the organi-zation can become rather creative about the problems it would like some other level of the organization to solve. In all of this the role of problem solver has skyrocketed as a dominant need for institutional leaders.

Movement Roles

As The United Methodist Church expresses its wish to become more of a Wesleyan movement it is asking for different roles from its leaders. We are looking for our lay leaders, our clergy, our district superintendents, our general agency staff, and our bishops to become much more like catalysts and champions, helping to get new initiatives started and then setting them free rather than directing and developing legislation about how things should be done.

As I work with people on reframing their leadership there are four roles that seem most able to capture the movement nature that we desire as a denomination. While this is my summary list of roles, it comes from a reflec-tion on the work of others who are asking deep questions of themselves in the areas of responsibility to which they have been called, appointed, or elected. These more catalytic and championing roles that are linked to move-ment life include storyteller, mission strategist, supervisor, and resource director.

Storytellers

Starfish organizations live with ideology at the center. Denominations, which are intentional faith communities, live with their own form of ideo-logical center shaped by their theology and their faith story. For too long our congregations, conferences, and agencies have been telling weak stories focused on problems as they recount their histories. What is needed, and what is natural to a movement, is a bold, strong story about what needs to be different and why we are called to be the people to make that difference in the future. Movements need storytellers, people who can tell the bold story of what can be and what is intended to be and then point to the connection to Scripture and the encounter with Christ in our lives. Storytellers are people who, in the midst of problems or doubts, can retell the strong, bold story that will make us want to try again and risk something new because it connects with our purpose. They are people who can take our daily disciplines, practices, and chores and teach us how they connect with God's dreams for what could be. While we are so often worried about the what and the how of ministry, movements depend upon leaders who can tell us the story reminding us of the why.

Mission Strategist

Instead of institutional providers, movements need missional strategists who move to the balcony to get the bigger picture connected to purpose. In the local church when so many leaders get focused on membership, budget, and institutional vitality (or viability), the pastor or some key leader needs to step up to begin missional conversations about what Christ calls them to in that setting. When local churches are focused on their own programs and people, district superintendents need to move to the balcony to look at the full district mission field and then challenge individual congregations to take a piece of the action. Bishops need to be missional strategists over whole conferences and the general church so that activity at any and all levels is aligned with missional rather than institutional ends. If the world is to be transformed by individuals who are transformed into disciples, there have to be multiple integrated strategies developed, encouraged, and set free at all levels of the denomination.

Supervisor

The role of supervisor is the role of accountability as discussed earlier. It is sufficient to note that supervision is often accomplished by telling the person to be supervised in advance what question he or she will be asked to be accountable for later. When so many things compete for the attention and resources of our leaders it is the role of the supervisor to keep others focused on the core process—on keeping first things first. Supervision here is not a review of one's compliance to the standards and practices of the organization but accountability to the purpose. Movements tend to be rather free and inventive on how they move toward their purpose, but there is no lack of accountability for the end that is to be accomplished. Catalysts and champions do not direct how work is to move ahead, but they do help by initiating conversations that will move the work ahead, and they tell the bold story about why it is important to faithfully pursue such ends. As supervisors they continually ask others about what progress is being made and what is being learned that will shape next steps.

Resource Director

In established institutions those responsible for resources are most commonly given two roles. The first is to protect resources, and the second is to distribute resources according to tradition and in response to strongest need (which often means to direct vital resources to the part or parts of the system that are weakest and least able to support themselves). In contrast leaders of movements direct resources toward the outcome, the goal, the critically identified difference to be made. Movements are more comfortable accepting proximate losses for ultimate gains that encourage resources to be directed to those places and people where most gain can be garnered for the end desired. In catalytic fashion, resource directors in movements expend resources where something can happen, then they get out of the way. This fourth and final role of missional resource director may well be the most difficult, since it directly challenges the expectations and dependence of that part of us that is most traditional, most institutional, and most dependent.

A central and sustained attention to the core process of mission; a way to cut through the no's; equality at the table; catalytic and championing leaders—we are asking a lot of ourselves because these are all roles and practices not common to established institutions. However, I would argue that they are new roles and practices that live at the heart of our wish to be a movement. We don't just want to do ministry differently, we want to be missional, tied more closely to Christ than we are tied to Christ's church.

Can a Movement Live Inside an Institution?

Both are needed. The United Methodist Church needs to continue to be an institution because of its global size, the differences that it holds within itself, and its complexity of efforts, ministries, and programs. The United Methodist Church also needs to be a movement that captures the passion of people who are committed to making a difference, and moves with agility to meet a mission field increasingly differentiated by generational, geographic, and global niches and which is constantly morphing with the speed of technology. To be institution without movement is to be left behind. To be movement without institution is to be unstable and incapable of mounting a global response.

Institution and movement are not opposites in which one holds a truth that denies the other. It is not right to be one instead of the other. Rather than warring opposites, institution and movement are a polarity. A polarity, as defined by the work of Barry Johnson, is two equal and competing truths that must be held together in tension.[15] Should The United Methodist Church be institutional with a clear structure, established paths of communication, shared and distributed authority, and a body of rules and norms that guide the behavior of a widely diverse people? The answer is yes. Should The United Methodist Church be a movement capturing the passion of its origin, in which commitments to a changed life and to a just society drive all decisions and resource allocation so that, in the end, Christ's presence in people's lives makes a clear difference? The answer is yes.

Can The United Methodist Church wholly be both an institution and a movement at the same time? The answer is no. A polarity is two competing truths. Each of the truths is equally true but cannot be held together. Should any organization in today's global but flat world be organized, structured, complex but fully aligned? Yes, of course. Should any organization in today's global but flat world be agile, flexible, and immediately responsive to the changes in the marketplace? Yes, of course. Can any organization be fully organized and structured but also fully agile and flexible? No, to be fully one denies the ability to be fully the other.

The appropriate response to a polarity, in which there is truth on both sides, is not to choose which side to be on but rather to manage the tension that lives in the middle. To enable leaders to understand and manage the tension that exists between the two poles of a polarity, Johnson developed the "polarity map," a graphic tool to help leaders manage their experiences and their goals. A polarity map places the polar truths at opposite extremes but recognizes that there are strengths to be realized at each of the poles (the positive upside). The polarity map also recognizes that if a person or organization lives too closely for too long aligned only to one of the polar extremes, then the strengths realized in the positive upside will slip over time into the weaknesses of an overused strength (the negative downside). The basic form of a polarity map is as follows:

Polarity Map

| **P o l a r T r u t h # 1** | The upside: Positive benefits of being aligned with this particular left polar truth. | The upside: Positive benefits of being aligned with this particular right polar truth. | **P o l a r T r u t h # 2** |

POLAR OPPOSITES

| **P o l a r T r u t h # 1** | The downside: Problems experienced when one lives too closely for too long aligned with the left polar truth, which then produces the weaknesses of an overused strength. | The downside: Problems experienced when one lives too closely for too long aligned with the right polar truth, which then produces the weaknesses of an overused strength. | **P o l a r T r u t h # 2** |

Polarities are managed, not solved. Leaders function best when they are clearly aware of the characteristics of each of the quadrants of a polarity, positive and negative, so that neither of the opposing strengths is practiced to the extreme that will produce the negative of being overused. Polarity management teaches leaders to be aware of the quadrants so that when too many of the downside, negative characteristics on the right pole are being experienced, the leader can begin to develop the upside, positive characteristics of the left pole to counterbalance the weakness. Similarly, when the left pole becomes overused and begins to develop the downside, negative characteristics, the leader can begin to develop the upside, positive characteristics of the right pole to counterbalance the weakness. The appropriate response to a polarity is not to choose which side is right to the denial of the opposing truth but rather to manage where one is on the polarity map at any one time in an effort to maximize the upper quadrant strengths of both poles. This offers explanation for why organizations routinely and continuously move from centralized to decentralized forms, from spiders to starfish and then back again, by repetitive series of strategic planning or restructuring. Rather than just "moving deck chairs on the Titanic" as many complain about, the continual adjustments may well be efforts to manage the polarity of equal but opposing truths by which an organization must live.

Below is a polarity map describing the tension between institutions (spiderlike, centralized organizations found on the right side of the map) and movements (starfishlike, decentralized organizations found on the left side of the map). This is the polar tension of equal but opposing truths that the United Methodist denomination, along with her sister mainline denominations, currently faces.

Polarity Map

Decentralized

– agile
– creative
– empowering to individuals
– lots of new programs /
  initiatives
– something for everyone
– sense of experimentation
– comfort with failure
– entrepreneurial
– freedom to think beyond
  narrow practice

– structured
– organized
– team alignment
– collaborative
– resource alignment
– leadership accountability
– strategic
– formative supervision

POLAR OPPOSITES

Centralized

– unstructured
– chaotic
– individuals unconstrained
– competition over resources
  and attention
– unconnected silos
– impulsive
– no supervision or accountability
– unable to make choices
– diffuse and de-energizing
– lack of follow through

– rigid
– constraining
– evaluative
– summative supervision
– self-contained and
  competing silos
– unable to think or act
  beyond established plans

The United Methodist Church, like many other organizations and institutions, fared well following World War II by adhering closely to the right pole of a centralized organization. Highly structured and organized initiatives by a denomination that was fully aligned through polity spawned a season of rapid growth that accompanied the orderliness and growth of the surrounding culture of that post-war era. However, beginning in the 1960s, as the mission field changed, the overused strengths of an organized and structured centralized denomination increasingly produced the negative downside effects that have been haunting us and that do not change by looking for fix-its for our failure to keep pace with the changing mission field. The current interest and pressure to recapture the denomination as a Wesleyan movement is our effort to rebalance ourselves by introducing the upside of the left, decentralized characteristics that are more resonant with movements than they are with institutions. I do not believe that The United Methodist Church is seeking to divest itself from its institutional strength and capacity to be a global church. We are, however, seeking to escape the rigidity and limits of being overcentralized, overregulated, and overinstitutionalized. Ours is a story in which we do not need David to defeat Goliath but need for them to live harmoniously with each other. This is a remarkable challenge for leaders.

CHAPTER SEVEN

THE NEW WESLEYAN MOVEMENT

If we are to be a movement, we will need to take seriously what movements require. Movements that are without commitment and sacrifice aimed at making significant changes are easily reduced to mere slogans and T-shirts. As I hear the language of movement being used more broadly across the church, I believe that the ferment that is building in the mainline church and in The United Methodist Church is asking more of us than marketing.

The thrust of the original Wesleyan movement was to reform the nation, particularly the church, and to spread scriptural holiness over the land. The energy that is building around the new Wesleyan movement in North America is, as noted earlier, first focused appropriately on reforming the church. The nation surely needs to be reformed, and scriptural holiness is markedly absent in many places we look. However, the reality within the mainline church is that to effect such change in the nation will first require a reformation of the church itself. We will first have to relearn our real purpose and how to connect to the changed mission field.

Movements, like other ways in which humans organize themselves, have life cycles that need to be reenergized after time if the purpose of the movement is to remain viable. Movements begin with insight and deep conviction that something could and should be different or better. The beginning is fueled with a passionate ideology, clear ideas, and deep passion. From a small group the movement builds through several levels of the recruitment of followers. At the outset, movements are not well organized beyond rudimentary alignment around purpose and principles. However, as a function of growth, time, and the achievement of goals, movements become intentionally structured, progressing toward a stage of institutionalization.

Institutionalized movements become very organizational in practice and eventually place efficiency over effectiveness. Over time the process and practices of the organization become more important than the product originally intended by the movement. Renewal demands that the natural life cycle that results in institutionalism be interrupted and that a new, clear, and passionate beginning be found that can galvanize followers to again address needed change. Movements need to find ways to restart their focus and passion, or they will die a quiet death. This is the challenge that The United Methodist Church currently faces as we push toward a new chapter of life as a renewed movement.

The simple definition of a movement used in this book is a group of people who consciously and at their own risk connect to change the *status quo*. At the beginning of a movement, the number of people involved does not have to be large. I am taken by Margaret Wheatley's observation that every revolution that changed the fate of humanity started as a conversation between two people.[1] But as the conversation grows, more people become involved, the target of the movement becomes clearer, and goals of change become embedded. I would argue that the current development of a Wesleyan movement within The United Methodist Church is a convergence of smaller conversations that already have moved us out of despair and toward action. Some of these conversations were highly public events such as the 2007 Lake Junaluska convocation that gathered 850 leaders of the church from across the globe. Some of the conversations were smaller and more private as bishops and cabinets faced the reality that business could not be continued in familiar ways in their conferences. Some conversations were even smaller and quieter as leaders of congregations sought to remain United Methodist but began to shift their attention from institutional to missional focus. A common observation about movements is that they don't actually begin to organize and blossom until the desired change they seek already begins to happen and people see the hope of getting involved and pushing the change ahead. If this is the case then the good news for our United Methodist Church is that the current push to be a movement is a measure of the hope and conviction that began in small and initially dis-connected conversations but which now already lives within a growing number of United Methodists.

What Kind of Movement?

There are different kinds of social movements. David Aberle provides one of the most influential classifications of social and religious movements by using measures of how much change (limited or radical) is expected from whom (specific individuals or everyone).[2] In the case of the United Methodist movement a limited amount of change is expected from everyone, a form identified by Aberle as a "reformative social movement." The change expected is limited because what is sought is not the discontinuance or replacement of the institution but rather the bending of current practice and orientation to become much more missional. Congregations are expected not to cease worship services or to reorient themselves radically but to bend their worship practices to impassion people for discipleship and mission (personal piety and social holiness). Congregations and conferences are being urged not to cease committee meetings and governance but to bend these practices to refocus on changing people's lives and communities rather than focus on sustaining (or saving) the institution of the church. Bishops are being encouraged not to stop making pastoral appointments but rather to reshape their strategies of appointment making to serve the mission field and to give particular attention to both congregations and clergy who hold the greatest potential for making disciples. The denomination is not to be dismantled. However, the practices of the denomination are to be reconsidered and reoriented toward missional rather than institutional ends.

The target audience of the United Methodist movement is everyone—to the degree that people can be invited and not required to participate in a movement. We all have skin in the game. Everyone from local church participants to bishops and general agency secretaries is being challenged to rethink purpose. Leaders are being asked to reform practice to align with the new goals of disciple making and a transformed world. Since the changes desired cannot be directed, only designated, the widespread involvement of everyone is, in fact, what adds interest and intrigue. There is no individual or office that has the overview or authority to be able to instruct all others in the changes that are to be made. Movements, and particularly movements that seek to engage everyone, cannot hope to be so directive as to determine actions in all situations. But goals are set out, principles are identified, and those who choose to engage the purpose of the movement are urged to become not just involved but also inventive. The kind of movement that The United Methodist Church seeks within itself is a reformative social movement in which we are not yet able to agree specifically on how the church must reform itself. We do know, however, that efforts toward our newly sensed mission of disciple making have, nonetheless, begun.

The Injustice Frame

In order for any movement to coalesce there must be a sense of injustice around which participants frame their goals. In order to make something right, there must be a shared perception of something wrong. In the large, revolutionary movements such as the civil rights movement or the women's movement, the injustice is writ large and easily recognized. The part of our faith that challenges such social injustices will go unchanged and constantly will be with us. There continually will be the "isms" of life in search of God's justice, such as racism and sexism. The contest between property rights and human rights will continue as people fight over access to and control of resources in ways that leave some as have-nots behind the winning haves. Hatred that breaks apart families and leads nations to genocide will not fully abate. Such is the nature of sin. If death and taxes are the only things that we believe to be sure, then the sin of injustice can be added to the list to complete the unholy trilogy. Injustice as such must always be opposed. Paraphrasing Bill Coffin, just because Jesus said we are to love our enemies does not mean that we should not have any.[3]

The current effort in our church is the development of a less impassioned movement focused not on the deeper nature of sin but on spiritual dissatisfaction. There is a clear sense that something is wrong, something is missing, or is less than it was meant to be. In order for the movement to form and to recruit participants we need to nurture this growing awareness of that which is not right—of how we are not relevant, not sustainable. The good news of the current moment is that the awareness of both what is wrong and the sense that what we currently do is unsustainable is growing. Something must happen. If intentional change is not created by people reordering themselves around missional purpose, then unintentional change will happen by default as the old dies off, perhaps replaced by nothing. Robert Quinn simply notes that when an established organization or institution has separated itself from its purpose and its environment there are only two choices, either deep change or slow death.[4] The injustice of what is institutionally wrong in the mainline church is now more broadly acknowledged and understood.

This sense of institutional injustice and unsustainability fuels a movement because the issues that we face cannot be addressed as problems for which there are clear solutions. If, in fact, there were clear solutions to our issues, surely someone would have by now applied the solutions, and the problems would have been corrected. Our challenge is much more adaptive than can be addressed by problem solving. Instead we are being challenged to identify and change values, assumptions, and behaviors that have allowed the wrongs to continue. We are challenged to find new ways to be church, to be denomination.

A measure of how far we have already come in the development of a movement is the number of people within the denomination who are aware of and articulate about the situation of the denomination but are not hopeless or despairing. People are discomforted but, where once they were disempowered and felt a sense of failure, there now is a growing sense of energy, conviction, and empowerment leading people to feel that there is hope. One leader in the movement has suggested that, indeed, this is the presence of the Holy Spirit stirring the waters in which our church can be healed. More and more people have learned the particulars of our institutional injustice frame and now, articulate about that which is wrong, are energized to find that which is so much more right.

A Movement People—Beginning with Changes in Entrepreneurialism

Reflections by Jim Collins on the changes in the meaning of entrepreneurial leadership over the past thirty years offer insight into the leadership needed in the United Methodist movement.[5] He points out that entrepreneurialism initially referred to a person who risked following his or her own vision. The focus of entrepreneurialism was an idea. The entrepreneur was one who practiced a "weird black art" of organizational independence to go his or her own way in pursuit of a driving idea. Most important at this stage of entrepreneurialism was the sense that this form of leadership was a temperament—it was a condition of someone's personality deeply engrained in some and nontransferable to others. The idea of the need for such entrepreneurs began to show up as early as the 1980s in the literature about the mainline church as writers began to call for going beyond managing institutional rigidness to taking risks for missional change that would redirect the denomination. New leadership was called for. Recruitment and certification processes of mainline denominations were criticized for providing leaders too managerial and insufficiently entrepreneurial.

Collins, however, points out that the early understanding of entrepreneurs matured beyond the idea of a lonely individual leader with uncontainable personal attributes. It became clearer that entrepreneurialism was a learnable skill. Not limited to personality characteristics, an individual could be taught ideas, strategies, and practices that would make him or her entrepreneurial. Indeed, at this point in time, graduate business schools have courses and departments that teach entrepreneurial leadership as a formal discipline. If the first stage of understanding the entrepreneur was as a force of temperament or personality, this next stage focused on people who led good, then great, organizations. In his work on good to great organizations, Collins provided an overview of the ideas and practices that entrepreneurs must learn and implement.[6]

Collins then went on to identify a new stage of entrepreneurialism that is of particular importance to the discussion here. The new stage is entrepreneurialism as movement. He suggests that entrepreneurs are those who go from leading great companies to leading movements. A movement addresses the purpose or the idea that exists above and beyond the organization and for which the organization can offer support and direction. I would suggest that this sense of entrepreneurialism is the desire now felt in the mainline church to reach beyond the institution to reconnect to the purpose for which the institution exists. There are multiple examples in the corporate world of leaders reaching beyond organizational goals of profit to address ideals and issues that impact the local, national, or global community. Google is becoming deeply invested in wind-generated power technology not because this technology is necessary for its own corporate performance but because it is congruent with Google's values and its vision for an alternative future. Tom's of Maine sells toothpaste as a corporate product but has gone to great lengths and expense to offer a fully natural product, indeed a whole line of natural toothpastes, deodorants, and body soaps, to address larger ideals of health and environmental sustainability. The Tom's of Maine website has a page on "Giving Back," which speaks of the goodness of helping others, a value not always connected with corporate performance.[7] Unrelated to Tom's of Maine is Tom's Shoes, a company committed to a goal that goes well beyond profitability—"for every pair you purchase TOMS will give a pair of new shoes to a child in need. *One for One*."[8] The company website includes a video that presents the need to provide shoes to impoverished children and seeks to solicit support for what is clearly a movement begun by the company. Collins proposes that entrepreneurs in the current culture are movement people. They seek to align with ideas and purposes that are greater than the products or services produced by their organization or corporation.

Where once the primary factor that separated entrepreneurs from other leaders or managers was their ability to take risks, the defining issue now is their ability to manage ambiguity. Does Tom's Shoes make shoes as a profit for investors or for a better world? While the answer clearly is both, ambiguity is created in the recognition that profit for the corporation and shoes for the needy are competing, or polar, values. Producing shoes of high cost that support giving free shoes to needy children does not fully serve the company's need for high returns. The ambiguity for entrepreneurial leaders is that they must be able and willing to hold competing values and truths in tension rather than choose one and give up on the other.

Such is the case with entrepreneurial leaders—movement people—in the mainline church. Here too ambiguity and competing values can be easily found. Should clergy be cared for and supported as leaders in the performance of difficult and stressful work? Yes, of course. Should clergy be expended for mission and deployed to areas where they best can provide missional leadership even if it is not a place that is most personally satisfying? Yes, of course. The ambiguity is that deployment officers such as bishops and district superintendents must hold these two equal truths in tension in order to address the purpose of the church and missionally manage the human resources of the church. Should local congregational leaders plan for the future survivability and stability of their churches by protecting their resources? Yes, of course. Should local congregational leaders expend their resources for the missional purpose of making disciples and transforming the world, since only through such passion and faithfulness will the church live? Yes, of course. Entrepreneurial leaders—movement people—must be willing to move into countless such questions that produce competing claims and hold the ambiguity that is the consequence.

Missional Recruitment and the Need Beyond Passionate Leaders

Does everyone need to be an entrepreneurial leader in order for the mainline church to change course and become more missional? It would seem that the answer is no. It does not take everyone to make an institution change course. Nor does the change of direction depend on the initiative of only the people with the most authority. Movements are more fluid and malleable than that. Movements are not hierarchical and, especially at the beginning, are more principled than organized. Movements more simply require those people who do have passion and new insights to talk with one another and to try new things.

Talking with each other is conversation, is the currency of change. Recall Wheatley's notion that every revolution that changed humanity started as a conversation between two people. While movements can start as simple conversations, it does matter a good deal what people talk about. The past decades in the mainline church have been difficult and confusing. In confusing times it is natural and inviting to talk about what is wrong and who is wrong. When in the wilderness it is easy to be a complainer. Complaining conversations do not make up a movement.

In programs of peer learning by officers in the military, it is clear that those in training are expected to be *contributors*, not *complainers*. It is an important and necessary distinction. There are those who will complain and remain passive, waiting for the institution to ease their burden and solve their problems. These are Block's "consumers." But there are also those who are contributors, people talking with one another not only of what is but of what could be and how to get there. These are Block's "citizens." Movements depend upon citizens talking with one another, willingly taking on entrepreneurial ambiguity and trying new things, including what has not been permitted in the past.

Not everyone will get involved. In fact, movements can be described in three sequential waves of the recruitment of participants. The first wave of recruits are those who are most impassioned and clear about both the need for change and the hope that there can be change. These are the true believers, and they seek each other out. They extend themselves beyond normal limits of authority and institutional thinking to take on risks for the sake of the purpose they serve. They risk sanctions and hand slapping, and in some cases, they risk a good deal more. It is this smaller group of movement people who initiate change not by organizing everyone into agreement about change but by forging ahead and demonstrating hope to others.

The second wave of movement people are those who observe what the first wave is doing, see the benefits of the change, and want to offer their support. Sometimes thought of as people who join a movement "because it looks good on the resume," these are people who recognize the importance of the change but have joined the conversation and the work at a later time or in a safer way that requires less risk. This second wave of recruits is critical because for change to be embedded there must be a tipping point, a critical mass of those who see, believe, and are committed to a new way.

The third wave of movement people are those who come to see the importance of the change that is occurring but who also realize that the change will happen—and that they will reap the benefits of the change—without requiring their involvement. This wave of recruits does not take risks; they may offer encouragement to others, but most importantly they do not oppose the change.

Three waves of recruits who join a movement suggest a fourth group of people. There are also those who don't share the vision of the movement, don't agree with it, or don't have energy for the projected change. It is easy to cast these people as "bad people" resisting and opposing a "good" change. Nonmovement people, however, do not always need to be cast as bad. They actually may be needed. When a long-established institution such as The United Methodist Church or other mainline denomination is facing deep change, there are some people who are, in fact, tasked with following and enforcing the standing rules and standards of polity, which is a necessary but nonmovement role. In other words it is their role, appointed or self-chosen, to protect and preserve old, known ways as a legacy or inheritance of great worth.

As noted earlier, deep change in an established institution requires rule breaking. So too do institutions require rule followers. Established institutions going through change also need some sense of stability, which is provided by rule following, rule followers, and even rule enforcers. These groups maintain sufficient stability to carry known truths ahead, to protect against those who see rule breaking as the easy way of not being held accountable, and to manage institutional protection while movements seek change. Exchanges between rule breakers and rule followers are how we determine what is of value to bring along from the past and what to jettison.

Moses took people into a wilderness in search of a new identity and a changed relationship with God. The wilderness is a chaotic and confusing place, messy rather than neat, creative rather than predictable. Movements do not introduce neatness and predictability into wilderness wanderings. But even then Jethro and Aaron were needed to impose some order and maintain some standards that would enable people to survive with some sense of stability in their lives.

The wilderness, movements, and deep change naturally put people against one another because of roles or temperament. Ambiguity suggests that there is usually some truth or some value in every position that people might take during times of change. Particularly when the deep change involves an institution of faith seeking a renewed purpose, it is critical that people, regardless of their position, treat each other well. Wherever we are, with whatever wave of recruits we stand with or stand apart from, we need to honor each other as children of God. The best of possible motives needs to be attributed to those who do not agree with us. Differences need not be directed or taken personally. Movements are about purpose, about the mission.

The United Methodist Church is not a unified institution if unity is defined by agreement. As in any large, complex organization with a history involving a broad range of participants across geographies, across varying life experiences, and across philosophical and theological preferences, there cannot be agreement to hold people together, only trust. Yet trust, while required in authentic relationships, is sufficiently fragile to demand risk if it is to be the necessary foundation on which community is built.

We are a church that would be a movement. The risks are great. The challenges are significant. The amount of new learning needed is mountainous. But the good news is that the movement has already begun. What is asked now is for more citizens to step forward leaving their consumer selves behind.

NOTES

1. We've All Got Skin in the Game

1. See Gil Rendle, "Leadership Under Constraints," www.tmfinsti tute.org/documents/resources/leadership_under_constraints.pdf.

2. What Holds Us Together

1. Gil Rendle, *Journey in the Wilderness: New Life for Mainline Churches* (Nashville: Abingdon Press, 2010).

2. *The Book of Discipline of The United Methodist Church* (Nashville: The United Methodist Publishing House, 2008), 41-42.

3. Ibid., 45.

4. Ibid.

5. Ibid., 46-47.

6. Ibid., 48.

7. Ibid., 54.

8. Craig Dykstra and James Hudnut-Beumler, "The National Organizational Structures of Protestant Denominations: An Invitation to a Conversation," in *The Organizational Revolution: Presbyterians and American Denominationalism*, ed. Milton Coater, John Mulder, and Louis Weeks (Louisville: Westminster John Knox Press, 1992), 307-31.

9. Russell Richey, *Extension Ministers: Mr. Wesley's True Heirs* (Nashville: General Board of Higher Education and Ministry, 2008), 23-24.

10. Robert Quinn, *Deep Change: Discovering the Leader Within* (San Francisco: Jossey-Bass, 1996), 91.

11. *The Book of Discipline*, 87.

12. Gil Rendle, "Welcoming 'Time Share' Christians," *Circuit Rider* 33, no. 1 (Nov/Dec/Jan 2008–09): 14-16.

13. *The Book of Discipline*, 45.

3. Breaking Rules

1. Thomas Kuhn, *The Structure of Scientific Revolutions*, 2nd ed. (Chicago: The University of Chicago Press, 1970), 52-76.

2. *The Book of Discipline of the United Methodist Church*, 160.

3. Peter Block, *Community: The Structure of Belonging* (San Francisco: Berrett-Koehler, 2008), 63.

4. It's Time to Testify

1. Tom Long, *Testimony: Talking Ourselves into Being Christian* (San Francisco: Jossey-Bass, 2004), 6.

2. William Sloane Coffin, *Credo* (Louisville: Westminster John Knox Press, 2004), 10.

3. Mary Walton, *The Deming Management Method* (New York: Perigee Books, 1986), 22-32.

4. Reggie McNeil, *Missional Renaissance: Changing the Scorecard for the Church* (San Francisco: Jossey-Bass, 2009).

5. "A Covenant Prayer in the Wesleyan Tradition," *The United Methodist Hymnal* (Nashville: The United Methodist Publishing House, 1989), 607.

6. John Wesley, "Catholic Spirit," text from the 1872 edition. Based on 2 Kings 10:15 Wesley wrote: "I mean lastly, love me not in word only, but in deed and in truth. So far as in conscience thou canst (retaining still thy own opinions, and thy own manner of worshipping God,) join me in the work of God; and let us go hand in hand" (section 2, paragraph 7).

5. Citizenship in the Movement: Voting Against One's Self-Interest

1. Jim Collins, *Good to Great and the Social Sectors: A Monograph to Accompany Good to Great* (www.jimcollins.com, 2005), 4-6.

2. Tony Wagner, *The Global Achievement Gap* (New York: Basic Books, 2010), 154-57.

3. Robert Quinn, *Deep Change: Discovering the Leader Within* (San Francisco: Jossey-Bass, 1996), 91-92.

4. Nancey Murphy, *Beyond Liberalism and Fundamentalism: How Modern and Postmodern Philosophy Set the Theological Agenda* (Harrisburg: Trinity Press, 1996).

5. Arthur Schopenhauer, *Parerga and Paralipomena: Short Philosophical Essays*, vol. 2, trans. E. F. J. Payne (Oxford: Xlarendon, 1974), 651-52.

6. Sally Dyck and Annie Arnoldy, "Holy Conferencing: Unity amid Diversity," *Circuit Rider* 35, no. 2 (Feb/Mar/Apr 2011): 10-11.

6. Can David Live with Goliath? Can a Movement Live Inside an Institution?

1. Ori Brafman and Rod Beckstrom, *The Starfish and the Spider: The Unstoppable Power of Leaderless Organizations* (New York: Penguin Group, 2006).

2. Gil Rendle, *Journey in the Wilderness: New Life for Mainline Churches* (Nashville: Abingdon Press, 2010).

3. Brafman and Beckstrom, 95.

4. Edwards Deming, *Out of Crisis* (Cambridge: Massachusetts Institute of Technology, 1992), 4-5.

5. Brafman and Beckstrom, 20.

6. Ibid., 67.

7. Eddie Gibbs, *Churchmorph: How Megatrends Are Reshaping Christian Community* (Grand Rapids: Baker Academic, 2009), 12.

8. Ibid, 121.

9. Brafman and Beckstrom, 88.

10. Ibid., 90.

11. Tom Porter, *The Spirit and Art of Conflict Transformation: Creating a Culture of Just Peace* (Nashville: Upper Room Books, 2010), 81.

12. Brafman and Beckstrom, 92.

13. Ibid., 100.

14. Gil Rendle, "Leadership Under Constraints," www.tmfinstitute. org/documents/resources/leadership_under_constraints.pdf.

15. Barry Johnson, *Polarity Management: Identifying and Managing Unsolvable Problems* (Amherst: HRD Press, 1992).

7. The New Wesleyan Movement

1. Margaret Wheatley, *Turning to One Another: Simple Conversation to Restore Hope to the Future* (San Francisco: Berrett-Koehler, 2002), 3-5.

2. David F. Aberle, *The Peyote Religion among the Navaho*, 2nd ed. (Chicago: University of Chicago Press, 1982), 315-22.

3. William Coffin, *Credo* (Louisville: Westminster John Knox Press, 2004), 152.

4. Robert Quinn, *Deep Change: Discovering the Leader Within* (San Francisco: Jossey-Bass, 1996), 5.

5. Jim Collins, "How to Thrive in 2009," *Inc.*, April 1, http://www.inc.com/magazine/20090401/in-times-like-these-you-get-a-chance.html (accessed March 25, 2011).

6. Jim Collins, *Good to Great* (New York: Harper Business, 2001).

7. See www.tomsofmaine.com/community-involvement (accessed November 21, 2010).

8. See http://www.toms.com/?keyword=tom's%20shoes&network= g&matchtype=e&mobile=&content=&search=1&gclid=CJ67kueE7acCFQY6 5Qodyg4wcA (accessed March 15, 2011).

CPSIA information can be obtained at www.ICGtesting.com
Printed in the USA
LVOW010612291211

261469LV00003B/3/P